ENGLISH
FOR
EVERYBODY

ENGLISH
FOR
EVERYBODY

ELLSWORTH BARNARD

The Dinosaur Press

Amherst

Copyright © 1979 by Ellsworth Barnard

All rights reserved
Library of Congress Catalog Card Number 79-18238
Printed in the United States of America
Library of Congress Cataloging in Publication Data
appear on the last printed page of this book.

The Dinosaur Press
Box 372   Amherst Massachusetts 01002

For Russell Thomas
who I hope will approve

CONTENTS

Preface ix

Part One. Usage and Grammar

1. Introduction 3
2. Usage 16
3. Grammar 41
4. Change 58

Part Two. Style

5. Clarity 79
6. Naturalness 97
7. Forcefulness 106
8. Beauty 120

Epilogue. On Teaching and Learning the Use of English Prose 129

Index 137

PREFACE

Generally speaking, non-fiction prose works are of three kinds: popular books, scholarly books, and textbooks. The present work, however, is none of these. Though I hope some parts may be entertaining, entertainment is not the purpose. Though I hope the ideas are sound, they are not original, nor based on exhaustive research. Though students may find it useful, it does not pretend to offer the "right" answers to all the specific questions that confront the person who wishes to write well.

What the work does do, if it fulfills its author's intention, is state clearly and illustrate convincingly a thesis that, though stated many times before, is often misunderstood and often disputed: that in the use of language there are no absolutes, but that rightness is relative to the user, the subject, and the audience; and that all these exist in relation to a particular time, place, and culture, and are therefore subject to change.

The conviction that there is still a need to restate this thesis, though to professional linguists it may seem threadbare, is in part the result of many years of trying to help college students learn to use their language well. It was reinforced by the widespread and impassioned response to a brief informal statement that I made some time ago that happened to catch the public eye; by the furor that greeted the publication of *Webster's Third New International Dictionary*; by the rejection of the thesis, still, by the "panel of experts" assembled by the editors of the *American Heritage Dictionary* to pass judgment on matters of usage; and by the fact that "some of my best friends" still adhere to a view of language that seems to me not only out of keeping with the obvious facts but confusing and discouraging to many students, in and out of classrooms, who are earnestly struggling to master their native tongue.

Though the thesis itself is not new, the illustrations are current—from newspapers, magazines, and TV programs. Many of them are from the Boston *Globe* and the *New York Times*—simply because these are what I read. It would be unfair, I am sure, for readers who reject my views to conclude that these publications have lower standards of literacy than the press in general.

The number of illustrations could easily have been multiplied. In fact, many usages that are unacceptable to what I call the "absolutist" view are so common that to give examples would be a waste of time. On the other hand, the judgments I offer concerning the status of some particular items are admittedly subjective, and I may sometimes be in error in my estimate of which of two competing grammatical forms is used more often, or which of two conflicting meanings of a word is dominant. Such errors, however, if they are judged to exist, do not affect the general thesis.

The first part of the book is concerned with what is "correct"—that is, what is *appropriate* because, in a given situation, it is commonly used. But what is acceptable is not always what is best, and the second part of the work suggests some qualities of style that—in general and not necessarily in every piece of writing—contribute to success in communication, which is the only function that language has.

The ideas in these essays have come from many sources, in ways that cannot now be traced, and I am not conscious of any particular debt that needs to be acknowledged, though I know of many published works in which similar ideas have been expressed. I trust the authors of these works, should they happen to encounter this restatement of principles that they had stated before, will accept it as an independent confirmation of their views.

ONE
USAGE AND GRAMMAR

1
INTRODUCTION

How should the English language be spoken and written? Few issues draw from middle-class Americans a more impassioned response. They may know little of linguistic theory, they may know little about how they themselves actually speak, but they know how they want their fellow Americans to use the language. The person who challenges the rules of "grammar" that they learned so painfully from high school teachers and textbooks—perhaps detested then but revered in retrospect—incurs their vehement and vocal resentment.

Let an innocent teacher of English, for example, tell a group of other teachers of English a few facts about actual usage (facts long since commonplace among informed students of the language); let him rashly repeat the statement to a reporter from the United Press; and he finds himself a public enemy, bidden by anonymous correspondents to "drop dead," satirized in the public press and in private letters in effusions of studied illiteracy ("Prof Says Bum English Ain't So Bad After All," chortled a headline writer for the *New York Times*), and scourged by editorial writers across the land as a "traitor to his profession," guilty of a "horrifying . . . incitement to mob rule."

What would be *really* horrifying, if anything connected with language could be so to one who has spent forty-odd years teaching college English, is the ignorance on the part of many English teachers, editorial writers, and other presumed shapers of the nation's verbal taste, of the most elementary facts about the nature of language, and the resolve of these persons to retain their blissful state.

What were the statements that raised so many people's blood pressure? One was: "Anything is all right if it fits the occasion and expresses the intended thought." Another was that nobody need worry about the textbook rules concerning "I" and "me," "shall" and "will," and "who" and "whom." Yet such statements have been accepted for years by professional linguists; they are sanctioned in an increasing number of textbooks of composition for college freshmen; and they are in accord with the practice of many persons who possess intelligence and taste.

What may have given most offense was the comment, "Whatever is used, is right"; and this remark certainly needs to be explained. The whole article by the United Press reporter, in fact, even in its unmutilated form, was inevitably oversimplified, though faithful in intention. And after the mayhem committed on it by various editors, as well as the more excusable whimsies of the headline writers, most of the published versions displayed a brashness that invited rebuke.

But a more detailed and exact statement in the *New York Times Magazine*, containing only a couple of editorial distortions,[1] detonated another blast of disapproval. Some responses, it is true, expressed heartfelt agreement. But the prevailing note was clearly one of outrage. The author was accused of saying, in effect, "We are lowering our scholastic standards, our standards of dress, our moral standards; let's lower our standards of the language arts"; of offering "an apologia for the slovenly blend of gangster argot and Hollywood patois that passes for the English language in America"; of making "another attack in the campaign to create a dictatorship of the illiterate"; of giving "lectures ... on how to be slobs"; of doing "the teaching of English a grave injustice" by writing the "sort of article that causes poor, befogged, uninformed students to leap for joy."

This whole affair, of course, was only a minor skirmish in the

---

[1] One of these changes had an ironic result. I wrote, "I shudder at the thought of drilling children in such a construction as 'I thought it to be him' or 'It appears to be she.' " But somebody, for some unknown reason, changed "him" to "he." And no less than four correspondents, who obviously *had* been well drilled in such constructions, took me to task for not knowing the rules that I was attacking.

INTRODUCTION

continuing war between opposing schools of thought. Readers over thirty may recall the furious controversy that erupted with the publication of *Webster's Third New International Dictionary* in 1961. While few persons would assert that the work was above criticism, the most intense shock and anger were undoubtedly caused by the editors' adherence to the principle that the function of a dictionary is to describe and not to prescribe, and their refusal to deal in value judgments. Yet this position had been taken by the first great English lexicographer, Dr. Samuel Johnson, two hundred years earlier. Nobody has ever accused Johnson of being by temperament unduly permissive, but in dealing with language, he was a realist. Anticipating the kind of criticism incurred by *Webster's Third*, he observed, concerning different meanings of the same word: "Most men think indistinctly, and therefore cannot speak with exactness; and consequently some examples might be put to either signification; this uncertainty is not to be imputed to me, who do not form but register the language, who do not teach men how to think, but relate how they have hitherto expressed their thoughts."

What are the causes of these periodic explosions? Mostly, perhaps, the protests spring from insecurity, which hides its face behind various masks. One of these is snobbishness. Those who are worried about their status discover in the use of textbook English a relatively easy way to assert their superiority to the masses; and if eminent authors and other public figures regularly "break the rules"—as of course they do—this is still more flattering to the critic's ego. If it were pointed out to such a person that Winston Churchill said at least once (and probably often) "the reason . . . is because . . ." or that Queen Mother Elizabeth and Eleanor Roosevelt were both reported in the press as having said "those kind of . . ." (as Thomas Paine did in *The Crisis* two hundred years earlier), it would never occur to him that *his* standards might be invalid; he would only congratulate himself on the fact that the most famous and admired persons in the English-speaking world were capable of errors that *he* would never make.

Another form of insecurity, it must be said with regret, inspires the antagonism of many teachers of English. To be brutal, their problem is that if they did not spend so much time on mechanics and grammar, old style, they would not know how to fill up the class hour. "Drill" on "fundamentals" helps keep pace with the clock and keeps students from asking embarrassing questions. It also evades the obligation to deal with matters of organization and style (many students have told me, with every evidence of truthfulness, that almost no writing had been required of them in high school), which as they are vastly more important, are also vastly more difficult. For these demand reflection, these involve choice, these permit and compel the exercise of independent judgment. In this kind of work a teacher cannot so easily say to a student "This is right" or "That is wrong." If the class is not completely cowed or indifferent, some members will ask "Why?" And since no textbook can cover all the contingencies that arise in actual writing (it cannot cover all that might arise in grammar, either, but *there* a partial consistency makes it easier to exclude the subversive exceptions), the teacher must answer with ideas of his own, which he must then defend, instead of retreating behind an ancient Chinese wall of dogmatism.

From this compulsion to state and stand up for an independent opinion, many teachers recoil, because they, like much of the general public, are always reaching for the security offered by absolutes. They want the line between "right" and "wrong" to be always drawn with the utmost sharpness; their fear of disapproval makes them want to be told how they should dress, how they should hold their knife and fork, how they should conduct their sex life, what brands of cigarets or liquor they should choose in order to be "in"—and, somewhere along the line, how they should speak and write.

It is possible to sympathize with this urge to conformity, to which mass advertising, among other social compulsions, lends almost overpowering support. Yet the will to resist such pressures and make conscious decisions is, one may suppose, mainly responsible for both the material and moral advances (and there *have* been moral advances, here and there) of Western civilization.

Perhaps a still more potent cause of verbal conformity is mere habit and inertia. For generations, children in schools have been taught to accept "rules" whose validity is alleged to be absolute; and whether or not they have as adults observed these rules in their own speech and writing, it is a shock to find them publicly challenged, to be told that "correctness" is relative. Such a challenge shakes the foundations of their whole existence. It is more

INTRODUCTION

unsettling than an attack on motherhood, to which Women's Liberation has accustomed us, or on the flag, which the Supreme Court has ruled may be worn on the seat of one's pants. We recognize that motherhood may be an excuse for egotism, self-indulgence, and domestic tyranny (the Jewish mother is a literary joke); and that patriotism, as Dr. Johnson noted long ago, and as we may too easily observe in our time and place (we call it "national security" now), is "the last refuge of a scoundrel." But to defy the traditional rules of grammer and usage is still (except in professional meetings and publications) to invite a verbal "protective reaction" of the most violent sort.

The power of mere habit and convention in the use of words is perhaps most forcibly illustrated by the school-imposed attitude toward "ain't." So many generations of school teachers have hammered into the minds of their pupils that "ain't" is wrong—that is, vulgar and offensive, like blue jeans at a society wedding—that it is never used by "educated" or "professional" people. (It is hard to describe in a word the difference between those who say "ain't" and those who avoid saying it, but the difference is certainly there.) Yet it has an ancient and honorable linguistic lineage, it presents no problem of communication, it is perhaps more musical than "isn't" and comes more easily to the tongue, and the taboo against its use creates an impossible situation when we wish to ask a question using "I." We say, "She's a beautiful girl, isn't she?" "You're happy, aren't you?" but "I'm your friend ... ?"—what? "Am I not?" moves with such club-footed reluctance that only under conditions of the utmost formality or, rarely, for extreme emphasis would one even think of using it. Yet there is no alternative. People occasionally venture "Aren't I?" but this jars us because of the obtrusive disagreement between a plural verb and a singular subject. Perhaps what is really being said is "A'n't I?"—"A[m] n[o]t I?"—which might be a satisfactory solution. The trouble is that people simply do not think of the word in this way. At any rate, the practical effect of ostracizing "ain't" is to deny us a natural and convenient way of speaking.

To be sure, we often do not know why language changes occur,[2]

---

[2] When this was written, the energy crisis had just dictated a change to Daylight Saving Time; and although the system had been with us, in the summer, for half a century, many people suddenly began saying and writing

and we cannot prove that the banishing of "ain't" from "standard English" is due to the efforts of too conscientious teachers. "We should be so influential!" (to use a phrase that the fastidious will scorn, but in which I find a blend of skepticism, irony, and pleased but deprecatory vanity that is altogether delightful, and that could be conveyed in no other way). Still, "ain't" is always the word that is seized on first by would-be satirists; it is the red flag always waved in the face of propriety by editors naturally eager to stir their readers' emotions ("Good Grammar Ain't Good English" was the title given—without my previous knowledge—to an essay already sufficiently provocative); it is the shibboleth that divides the saved from the damned. And since there is no *reason* for such a widespread and intense aversion, one naturally concludes that it has been *learned*, that it is the result of conscious social pressure. (Of course, there is still the question, "Where did *this* come from?")

The presence of such pressure is also evident in the common feeling that language in itself—words in themselves, apart from what they say—may have a moral, or immoral, quality; that "right" and "wrong" have the same meaning when applied to words as when applied to action; that using "ain't" (our standing example) is like exposing oneself. Of course the obvious illustration is "four-letter words"; the functions or organs that they refer to are facts of life, which *have* to be referred to, and *can* be referred to in longer words without reproach, if not always without embarrassment. But convention has decreed—at least until recently—that the four-letter terms must not be spoken in mixed middle-class company nor put in print before the public, even in fictional or dramatic works where they might be thought essential to the honest portrayal of character. It is often asserted, with an anger obviously genuine, that people's thoughts and conduct will be corrupted by seeing them in print. Older readers will remember the furor aroused by the one-time best seller *Strange Fruit*. That the author, Lillian Smith, was a Southern lady with impeccable social credentials did not lessen the outrage of readers who found a character using what for him would have been the only possible word for sexual intercourse.

"Daylight Savings Time." On one news broadcast, although the reporter said "Daylight Saving," the screen had "Daylight Savings." The change makes no sense, and I am annoyed by the assault on a habit and expectation of fifty years. Whether the new form will become established, remains to be seen.

INTRODUCTION

That uproar now—to a dweller in a university community, at least—seems infinitely remote. But it was rudely recalled toward the end of 1973, when the school board of a middle American small town, till then unheard of by the world at large, achieved momentary fame of a sort by publicly burning Kurt Vonnegut's *Slaughterhouse Five*, assigned to a high school English class by a teacher apparently unfamiliar with the mores of rural North Dakota. One gathered from the news accounts that this summary execution was carried out because a student protested to the board—whose members admitted that they had not read the book—against the presence of those same four-letter words.

This episode in turn calls to mind the semi-dirty story, dating from the forties, about a novelist and the editor of a Boston publishing house, who were discussing the manuscript of the former's latest work. The novelist, who was evidently something of a free spirit (after all, Ernest Hemingway, for all the hair on his chest, had resorted in *For Whom the Bell Tolls* to an awkward and self-conscious evasion of the problem), had had no qualms about putting into the mouths of his male characters (who may have been in the Armed Forces) the language that such men would really use; while the editor, being from Boston, was not only mindful of the probable reaction of the Watch and Ward Society and of the Boston Police Department, but could not read the words himself without a slight inward cringing.

He therefore hesitatingly confessed his misgivings to the author, at the same time assuring him of his enthusiasm for the work as a whole. And the novelist, who was neither disposed to magnify the objection into an affront to his artistic integrity nor concerned about the possible loss of readers who might have been attracted by the naughty words, was willing to be accommodating. "Just tell me what the words are," he said, "and I'll see what I can do about taking them out."

"Oh, I couldn't *tell* you," said the editor with a blush, "but I'll write them down on a sheet of paper"; and this he did.

The novelist questioned the need of removing *all* the words, and before complete agreement was reached, it was time for lunch. When the two men returned, they noted the precipitous departure from the vicinity of the editor's desk of several tittering office girls; and the editor was presently horrified to discover, not only that he had left the list of words in plain sight on the top of his desk, but that it was on a sheet of paper that he had previously headed, "Things to do today."

The hilarity with which this story was always greeted, by a wide variety of mixed audiences (to be sure, they were always English teachers) was never, as far as I could observe, qualified by either incomprehension or embarrassment. Everybody knows what the four-letter words are; and nobody (I would have said before the news from North Dakota) is ashamed of this knowledge.

So what we are faced with in the taboo against four-letter words, and against "ain't" and a host of kindred forms used by ordinary people in their everyday speech, is a false morality that confuses "right" and "wrong" with "appropriate" and "inappropriate." The question is not of morals but of manners, not of laws but of conventions, not of truth but of taste. The proper analogy is with dress, as a critic of my *Times Magazine* article unwittingly suggested: "Dr. Barnard's approach leads us to believe that he teaches in a school which permits its students to attend class in T-shirts and dungarees." This of course implies a double delusion—that dress as well as language is related to morality.

It also illustrates how rapidly conventions change—conventions of all sorts. To be sure, even twenty years ago, T-shirts and dungarees in college classes were not widely regarded as signs of moral decadence; but I do recall that less than a dozen years ago, at the university where I was then teaching, women were supposed to wear dresses or skirts to class—no slacks!

Of course there are obvious reasons why, in particular situations, we might wish not to violate particular conventions, either of dress or language. But none of the reasons have even the most remote connection with morality.

Some objectors, however, are inspired by a genuine moral concern. To an editorial writer in the Cleveland *Plain Dealer,* and to several private correspondents, the statement, "Factory workers . . . don't talk like college professors, and . . . there is no reason why they should," seemed to stigmatize factory workers as an inferior social class. "Because a man works in a factory, is decent grammar to be denied him? We maintain that this is still America, where every man has a chance to develop, whether his father came over on the Mayflower, or two weeks ago!"

But this anger, though admirable, is misdirected. My point is, of course, that the language of factory workers is as "decent" as that

INTRODUCTION

of anybody else—and incidentally, that factory work is as honorable as any other kind. The unstated premise of the critic is that textbook English and social respectability automatically go together. One of the main purposes of this essay is to show that such a notion is mistaken.

It is no doubt true that the language of most "working people" is limited, and no one (I hope) would disagree with the author of a letter to the Cleveland *Press* who described herself as "an old-fashioned housewife of 30 with a five-year-old son who just entered school and who will some day become an honest plumber if she does a good job. But it would break her heart if he were not given the opportunity afforded by high standards of education, to perhaps become a poet or a statesman, if he has the inclination." Of course every school child should have a chance to become familiar, through his reading, with the full resources of the language, and to be encouraged, "if he has the inclination," to make these resources his own. Even if he becomes a plumber—or a garbage collector (for whom our false morality considers that plain term to be demeaning)—his life will be enriched by this achievement, so that his leisure pleasures may be less meager than those of persons addicted to snowmobiling or TV football. (Is this snobbishness of a different kind?) But still, one may doubt if a knowledge of "grammar" is the key to such a devoutly to-be-wished-for consummation.

For some other thoughtful critics, the challenge to traditional rules presents a different moral issue. Their concern for society is genuine, and their arguments are not frivolous. They see the departure from tradition in the use of language as in part a symptom and in part a cause of what they view as cultural decay. They are incensed by the gobbledygook of bureaucrats in the government, or the military, or business—or, for that matter, in education; they are nauseated by the false folksiness of TV and other advertising, and its attempt to appeal to "ordinary people" by using language ("like a cigarette should") that ordinary people are supposed to use. And they associate this lack of clarity and this lack of sincerity, both the careless and the calculated reliance on stale and poverty-stricken verbal formulas, with what might be called the linguistic pragmatism of some English teachers and lexicographers.[3] When someone

---

[3] Edwin Newman in *Strictly Speaking* presents an appalling and hilarious collection of pompous, vacuous, repetitious, and cliché-ridden utterances of public figures, recorded by the media.

USAGE AND GRAMMAR

says, "Usage determines correctness," or "What is used is right," they assume that that person approves of the kind of language that they detest, and that he does so because of a lack of taste, or a desire to gain popular attention, or an indolent surrender to a current trend.

This was no doubt the motive for the censure of my remarks (as they were reported in the press) by such serious and sensitive writers as E. B. White (I assume, since it appeared in the *New Yorker's* "Talk of the Town") and Clifton Fadiman in his column in *Holiday* magazine. And the latter (whom some of my generation will remember as the genial, witty, and knowledgeable master of ceremonies in the best of all radio quiz shows, "Information, Please") gave deeply felt expression to this attitude in response to my letter of explanation and defense. Among other things, I said that while I agreed that "a lot of radio and TV announcers and the people who write their scripts" were disgusting, "I imagine the English language will survive their onslaughts.

Mr. Fadiman replied: "Our disagreement is not on matters of linguistics, but on matters of social influence. Madison Avenue *vs* the English language is an *un*equal combat. The tradition that enables you to write so temperate, clear, and interesting a letter [I value this praise] is under *calculated* attack by the Levelers (they elected a President,[4] after all) and the English language will not survive their onslaughts."

"I fear we must disagree (I hope amicably) on your principle: usage makes it so. This is true, when the changes are either (a) natural (b) in the direction of force, clarity, richness. The usage today is (a) dictated from Madison Ave, Bway, Hollywood (b) in the direction of fuzziness, poverty, dishonesty."

"Usage makes it so" is a principle to be discussed in the next chapter. Here let me try to refute the assumption that underlay Mr. Fadiman's initial response, as well as the response of many others who reverence the English language; namely, that those who

---

[4] The President was Eisenhower, just elected to a second term, whose extemporaneous style, best described as invertebrate, led many parodists into temptation. Its amorphousness was dramatized by the verbal genius of his opponent, Adlai Stevenson, whose overwhelming defeat in two Presidential elections was indeed an ill omen for the English language.

accept this principle are in fact advocating anarchy; that in rejecting certain oft-repeated rules that do not correspond to actual usage, we are accepting the doctrine that "Anything goes."

The assumption, however, is mistaken. To say that standards of usage vary from time to time and place to place, and from one social level to another, is not to deny that for a particular writer or speaker, addressing a particular audience on a particular subject, standards *do* exist, and need to be met. And the recognition of this fact confronts the writer or speaker with a far more difficult task than if there were a set of hard and fast rules to be followed under all circumstances. Every word must be chosen, every sentence must be formed, to fit a special occasion. The writer or speaker will not sacrifice his own integrity, he will scorn pretense or affectation; yet he will not needlessly offend an audience that presumably he wishes to inform or persuade. He will simply keep asking himself as he goes along, "In this unique situation, what is the best way of saying what I have to say?"

The elaboration of this principle—that is, the question of a proper style—is reserved for later discussion. But before this introduction ends, there is one more topic to be taken up. When a person writes a book, he ought to ask himself, "Why?" Despite Mr. McLuhan's prophecies, the world is drowning in print. And on the present subject, what more is there to be said, especially by an amateur? Many reasonable and readable works, both scholarly and popular, have already been written concerning it. Many composition textbooks for college freshmen, even, take notice of the main ideas contained in the present essay. If a large part of the educated public remains unconvinced, why should a further effort be expected to change anybody's views? "Have they not Moses and the prophets?"

To be sure, controversy is fun. But writing a book is work. And what difference does it make, anyway?

In the first place, the controversy makes clear that—whatever their motives—people *care*. They may not understand how their language works, but they do not take it for granted. They do not wish it to be abused. And therefore one need not apologize for continuing the dialog about what constitutes "good English."

Moreover, having given one's days and nights, through many years, to the teaching of "freshman composition" (and having been fired from a prestigious college for—among other things—vehemently opposing the removal of freshman composition from the curriculum, and for telling older colleagues who complained of the burden of reading themes that "it went with the job"), one cannot be a fatalist. A teacher of composition does not know how his students learn to write, nor what part his own efforts may play. But he has seen many a student's writing unmistakably improve, even during one semester, and even with the writing of a few thousand words. People *can* change their habitual way of writing, and even of speaking—and change it for the better.

But what is "better"? Is it conformity to rigid rules which contradict what students see every day in the most respected publications, and hear every day from the most respected people? Do not such negative commandments in fact confuse the student? Will they not, if he is observant and independent (as we say we would like him to be), incline him to think of textbooks and teachers as dogmatic and dishonest? Or if he is docile and anxious to please (as many of us *really* want our students to be), will he not be likely, through fear of doing "wrong," to stress *form* (and *minor* matters of form) rather than substance? All teachers are familiar with the student who never "makes mistakes" but who never *says* anything, either, and is aggrieved because the composition receives a grade of "C." No doubt such a paper is more often the result of an unoriginal mind (one recalls the unkind but probably truthful answer of the English teacher to the student who asked what he must do to get an "A": "Be born again") than of misguided instruction. But at best, "drill" on "fundamentals" (which are often not fundamental at all) wastes time that could be well spent on other matters—such as choosing exact words and apt illustrations, putting sentences together so that the stress falls on the important part of thought, and arranging topics in a clearly connected sequence.

And then, of course, anybody who thinks he sees the "truth" naturally wishes it to be shared—freely, of course, and not through coercion—by those whose sight, he believes, is less keen or who are looking in other directions. I am bewildered and distressed that so many persons of intelligence and good will ("some of my best friends"), who share my desire to increase the number of Americans who use their language well, still hold to a point of view opposed to mine. It must be that, despite all the learned and lively, as well as the uninformed and merely angry, discussions that the subject has

INTRODUCTION

called forth, the facts have never been presented in such a way as to win general assent from reasonable people.

Such is the modest aim of the present work, which is intended to be an essay in understanding: an appeal to reason against unreason, to fact against prejudice, to experience against authority.

2
USAGE

"Without assumptions," as Cardinal Newman once remarked, "nobody can prove anything about anything." The basic assumption in this essay is that the primary function of language is communication. We do not ever really talk to ourselves; if we seem to, it is only because the audience is imaginary. If we do use words without thought of an audience—as when we damn the door of the medicine cabinet for being in the way of our head—the words we use have no particular content; a grunt or growl would do as well.

We need go no deeper into the immensely complicated topic of the nature of language and the meaning of meaning. Instead, we may proceed to the corollary that the only absolute criterion of "good" or "bad" or "right" or "wrong" in the use of language is success or failure in communication. What aids communication is always "right"; what hinders communication is always "wrong." All other "rights" and "wrongs" are conventional and therefore relative, since conventions change.

That is, if there were any value in trying to maintain clear distinctions in meaning between "shall" and "will" and "who" and "whom" and "lie" and lay," it would be right to defend these distinctions as long as any considerable number of people wished to maintain them. But since, first, few people outside of English classrooms and editorial offices ever think about them; and second, those who are aware of them are often confused; and third, there is no reason why anyone should pay attention to them, since the *meaning* is never in question; the only sensible attitude is to let nature (in these instances) take its course.

To characterize these beliefs and this attitude, I suggest the word "pragmatic"; and I would call the opposing position "absolutist." The latter has sometimes been called "traditional" or "purist." But it is traditional only in the schools, not in the wider world of letters and affairs; and "purist" implies fidelity to some original and perfect source—which in fact never existed. Both terms, also, are heavily laden with emotional overtones, approving or hostile according to the bias of the reader. But "absolutist" exactly fits; the opinion or person thus described does not appeal—not really, though the claim may be made—to either precedent or system. The contention is rather that language *ought* to be used in accordance with certain abstract and unchallengeable rules, whose validity is unaffected by considerations either of what is useful or of what is *used*. The absolutist says simply, "This is right" and "That is wrong." To offer but one example, a typical admonition concerns "different than": "Never use the phrase." [1]

For the opposite position, "pragmatic" seems equally appropriate. True, it has connotations, like "traditional" and "purist," that may be either pleasant or repellent. But it is based undeniably on experience, on the way the language *works* for those who use it; it claims kinship with the flow of words and actions in the world that most people regard as real.

If the distinction is still unclear, perhaps analogies from the realms of art and morals may help. Many persons approach painting and sculpture with the unshakable belief that visual art *must* be representational, that its primary aim is to "hold the mirror up to nature"—a nature that, though perceived in different ways by different artists, is always recognizable. All non-representational works are then regarded as irrelevant—as non-art—and all attempts at explanation or defense simply fail to register. On the other hand, there are many persons who are willing to define art more widely

---

[1] Sheridan Baker, *The Practical Stylist*, p. 90. This is in many ways an excellent manual of style, and has been widely used as a text in "Freshman English." Even some of the prescriptions and proscriptions in the chapter on "Usage" are commendable as matters of style. But the underlying assumption is in my view invalid, and the effect on students can only be pernicious.

as "anything that is *made* and gives *pleasure*," [2] and who, finding pleasure in works whose forms or colors apparently correspond to nothing in nature and exist only for their own sake, are ready to affirm that these works have a right to be called "art."

Perhaps a still more forceful instance of the absolutist attitude is manifested by those persons who oppose the ruling of the United States Supreme Court concerning abortion. It would surely be unfair to assume that the anti-abortionists are less sensitive than those whom they attack, to the economic and emotional stress, the moral and social degradation, that may result from unwanted births, and that bear not only upon the parents but often most heavily on the helpless and innocent victims of a world they did not ask to enter. But these are only relative evils, since they are measured only by human standards, whereas the "Right to Life" is absolute because ordained (its apostles believe) by God. Life is an absolute, and though the word as they use it may, to persons with pragmatic views, denote only an abstraction, to which it is meaningless to attach human values, they do not see nor hear nor understand the specific arguments and instances with which their critics would confront them. To these, they "close the valves of [their] attention / Like stone."

Returning to the use of language, it is obvious that the pragmatic view that communication is paramount does not in itself solve each particular problem. Conventions differ in different situations, and success in communication often depends on conforming to those that prevail in the audience that is addressed. For an educated person to say "Ain't it?" (to resort once more to our example for all occasions) in speaking to a college audience would shock most hearers—even those who themselves use the expression in campus conversation—into inattention to what is being said: whereas it would be equally out of place for a truck driver (no offense to truck drivers) in speaking to a group of his fellows, to say, "Is it not?" The resulting blockage in communication might be just as great. Even such generalizations, however, must be modified in particular instances, as when William Faulkner remarked to a group of students at the University of Virginia: "He [the author] ain't too interested in what the contemporary world thinks about him."

---

[2] I am speaking here only of the visual arts. A general application would perhaps require a narrower definition.

USAGE

Presumably the winner of the Nobel Prize for Literature found the word natural in informal speech and the students naturally accepted that fact.

Or take again our "four-letter words." Some people will be so outraged at seeing them in print that, if they do not stop reading altogether, their minds will simply fail to register the sense of the passage as a whole. And if the words were spoken to a typical "middle-American" group of persons of both sexes, the shock and hostility would perhaps be even greater. On the other hand, the writer of fiction and drama may feel that without using these words he cannot fully communicate the quality of the character or of the experience that he is trying to present. Moreover, the reader's shock at finding convention defied may, instead of paralyzing him, rouse him to a sharper awareness of the full meaning of the passage.

So much, then, for the basic assumption—that the function of language is communication. And if this function is to be performed, then both—or all—parties to the process have to agree on what words mean; and also, since meaning is determined by the total context, on how they are to be put together and how they are to be fitted to the unique relationship between the writer or speaker and his audience.[3]

The difficulty is that there is no science of language. In mathematics the ratio between the diameter and the circumference of a circle is always the same. The chemical formula for water does not vary. In genetics there are no exceptions to Mendel's law. But language is the expression of the human psyche, and this is something that nobody has yet been able, except in the crudest way, to measure or classify or confine. We stumble and fumble toward each other, making sounds and marking symbols that we hope will produce in the other person or persons an inner experience corresponding to our own. But the correspondence can never be more than partial, and the degree of our success is something that we can only guess at.

To be sure, we must always strive for certitude. We must never cease our efforts to scale or penetrate the barriers, to bridge the

---

[3] Pronunciation and spelling, in speaking and writing respectively, are also important, since deviations from what is expected distract the attention of the audience. But in these areas there is less controversy. Fewer persons (though still some) would challenge the proposition that "correctness" in spelling and pronunciation is purely conventional, that what is used is right.

gulfs, to dispel the shadows, that limit or distort the common ground of our experience. This must be the aim of all teachers and learners, especially in the realm of language. And one obvious means is to expand the area of agreement on how language should be used.

But this agreement cannot be dictated from above, by teachers or scholars or lexicographers. It is perhaps natural that these persons should wish to legislate concerning the use of language, as the same attitude was natural for the real or mythical legislator of a Midwestern state who noted the inconvenience arising from the value of *pi* and proposed to fix by law the ratio between the circumference and the diameter of a circle at exactly 3 to 1. But their attempts, though less obviously irrational, are confronted by a reality no less recalcitrant.

It may be true that the language as these authorities use it, and as they would require other people to use it, is a better instrument of communication—at least to other members of their particular group—than it is as used by the unthinking majority. But we in the academic community (for instance) do not want to talk only to each other. The business of the world is not transacted, the decisions that determine the course of our outward lives are not made, in professorial offices. If the scholar seeks an audience outside his own profession, if he acknowledges an obligation to a community not confined within academic walls, he must be, like Wordsworth's poet, "a man speaking to men."[4]

And we must use a language that will be understood by those we address. Though we speak with the tongues of men (and of women) and of angels, if the words we use have a different meaning for our audience than[5] for us, then we might better save our breath. It does

---

[4] Must we now say, in deference to Women's Liberation, "a person speaking to persons"? If not to do so involves cutting communications with half our prospective audience, no doubt we must, even at the cost of substituting a flat, blank, soporific expression for one that is resonant and arresting. The accepted convention has been that "man" in such a context implies not "maleness" but "human-ness"; and it is hard for a person more concerned with the effectiveness of language than with the propagation of an abstract ideology to understand how this convention can be regarded as degrading to the female sex. In regard to this issue, however, reason is apparently irrelevant, and a different convention is to be imposed.

[5] Some absolutists would demand that "than" be replaced by something like "from what they have." Is any comment needed?

not matter that we may have tradition and history on our side. If yesterday's meaning is not today's, then yesterday's is irrelevant. That useful distinctions may have been lost is also irrelevant. The question is, "Do we want to be understood, or not?"

A case in point is "flout" and "flaunt." Perhaps because "flout" (to defy) and "flaunt" (to display) are not only similar in form but carry the same suggestion of recklessness and disdain, inattentive readers and careless writers have slipped into the habit of using the latter in place of the former, and their example has been followed so often that it has now acquired respectability. An appeal for funds by the National Lawyers Guild, in joining the drive to unseat Richard Nixon, declared: "Despite overwhelming public outcry and criticism, Mr. Nixon continues to flaunt the law." Of course, some persons do not consider the National Lawyers Guild respectable. But would they say the same of former Mayor Lindsay of New York, who asserted (as quoted in the Boston *Globe*): "I shall not permit the public interest to be flaunted"? Well, perhaps they would. Certainly there are some who would deny respectability to the Planned Parenthood League of Massachusetts, which accused the anti-abortionists of "flaunting the Supreme Court decision." But, though I have not yet seen this usage attributed to Ronald Reagan, I doubt that it is only "liberals" who are guilty of it. It is my judgment, in fact, that "flaunt" now regularly means "defy" and "flout" is passing out of use. We may deplore the loss to the language, but we cannot change the fact that words mean what they are used to mean. (What is perhaps most unfortunate is that during the transition a careful writer will feel constrained to avoid using *either* of these once forceful terms.)

Or take "disinterested" and "uninterested." The latter once meant (and still means, when it is used) simply "not interested"— indifferent or uncaring—while the former usually meant "not *selfishly* interested"—that is, impartial or just, perhaps even with a suggestion of altruism, of acting against one's own interest narrowly conceived. A disinterested person was one who wished to see a situation exactly as it was; who would not, for instance, take sides in a quarrel, even though one party might be his friend, without understanding precisely what was going on, and on which side justice lay. But all this has evidently been forgotten. At a guess, nine persons out of ten (who read or write for, let us say, the *New York Times*) now think that "disinterested" means "indifferent"—and *therefore* it *does.*[6] No one, I suppose, would bring a charge of illiteracy against the author of the "Topics of the Times," for many years a feature of the editorial page of the Sunday *New York Times;* yet in a temperate discussion of the controversy that gave rise to the present work, he observed that "the language . . . is as much damaged by the unimaginative or disinterested use of it as by incorrect use." I myself am inclined to regret the loss to the language of "disinterested" in the traditional sense, for which there is no exact substitute; and there is no law forbidding us to use it in its former sense. But we shall not be understood.

A similar change has overtaken "imply" and "infer." When I was young, I understood that a speaker or writer "implied" something that he did not wish to say in so many words, and that the hearer or reader "inferred" what that something was. Even then, however, the change must have been under way, since the textbooks warned against confusing the words. And now, it seems, the speaker or the writer is the one who "infers"; nobody (almost) "implies."[7] Yet people still communicate. Words mean what the users think they mean. The English language is not destroyed by the principle "usage makes it so." New generations will adjust to change, and find new ways, if necessary, of saying what they wish to say.[8]

On the other hand, since we know so little of why changes occur, there is no reason to assume that any particular change of which we begin to be aware is inevitable. We may believe, instead, that until a certain point in the process has been reached, a trend may be reversed; and that when such a trend, as in the examples just cited, makes the language a less effective instrument of communication, we can and ought to, with good hope and in good conscience, op-

[6] The *Oxford English Dictionary,* that unique repository of English linguistic history, gives three early examples of "disinterested" in its present sense —in 1612, 1684, and 1767—which it labels "obsolete." The *Supplement* removes the label, and gives seven examples since 1928. Today any casual reader can find his own examples. Incidentally, Noah Webster in 1828 defined "disinterested" as "uninterested," though he added the traditional definition. He concludes with the bracketed comment: "This word is more generally used than 'uninterested.'"

[7] I have to except 92 per cent of the *American Heritage* Usage Panel. (See below.)

[8] Other examples of changed or changing meanings will be given in Chapter 4.

pose that trend. The difficulty is in deciding when such a point has been reached.

We can, of course, consult the dictionaries. But, for one thing, dictionaries are always out of date; the language has changed while they were being put together, and in some respects (like many weapons doted on by military planners) they are obsolete before they are ready for use.

And for another thing, the editor's personal bias may stand in the way of accuracy. A famous instance is Dr. Johnson's definition of "pension": "An allowance made to anyone without an equivalent. In England it is generally understood to mean pay given to a state hireling for treason to his country." "Pensioner" is similarly defined as "a slave of state hired by a stipend to obey his master." (One is happy to note that later, when a Tory government came to power and offered him a pension, he ignored his definition and accepted it!) In our own time, *Webster's Third* clearly reflects the linguistic philosophy of the editor-in-chief, Philip Gove. And while this philosophy is in my judgment generally sound, it leads to what I have to regard as a genuine defect—the refusal to recognize different "levels of usage," to acknowledge the importance of the social context.

The editors of the *American Heritage Dictionary* took note of the outcry against what seemed to many persons an evasion of responsibility, and introduced such labels as "Nonstandard," "Informal," and "Vulgar." Of course, these categories are still to some extent subjective, but they do correspond in general to unquestionable facts of usage. Moreover, in an attempt to strike a balance between what I have called "absolutism" and "pragmatism," they set up a panel of 105 persons to distinguish in particular instances between "standard" and "nonstandard" English; a task for which they were qualified by "the recognized ability to speak and write good English." An unfriendly critic might complain, of course, that "good English" begs the question, and might ask. "*Whose* 'good English'?" and " 'Recognized' by whom?" But even the most thorough-going pragmatist must acknowledge that both the concept and the phrase are instruments that anyone concerned with language simply cannot get along without.

Nevertheless, the cards are stacked. Only a few members of the panel are professional linguists. The rest, however varied their fields of activity—fiction, history, criticism, science, sports, the arts—are card-carrying members of the literary Establishment, and absolutists at heart. As Morris Bishop, author of the dictionary's admirable introductory essay, sound in substance and delightful in style, on "Good Usage, Bad Usage, and Usage," frankly admits: "they tend to feel that the English language is going to hell if 'we' don't do something to stop it, and they tend to feel that their own usage preferences are clearly *right*." Ninety per cent of them assert that "disinterested" is "not acceptable in the sense of 'uninterested,' though it is often thus employed." Ninety-two per cent refuse to admit that "infer" is taking the place of "imply." Sixty-six per cent reject "contact" as a verb. They never heard, apparently, of King Canute.

If such a distinguished panel cannot be trusted, a handbook expressing the taste of a single person is likely to be still more arbitrary, though in recent years some teachers of college English have taken a pragmatic position.[9] Fowler's *Modern English Usage* (1926) is looked on by many persons as a sort of Bible, and on many topics the author is both sensitive and sensible. But under the heading "Illiteracies" are listed several items that to my ear are perfectly acceptable. Such phrasings as "It looks as though we shall win" are unimpeachably standard. Three others—"Whatever can this mean?" "Though she had promised to write him soon . . ." and "I did not think to tell them"—I should use in conversation without a second thought (meaning without *any* thought). And two others—"like" as a conjunction introducing a subordinate clause, and the objective case in a gerund construction ("Instead of me being dismissed . . .") —are used so constantly, even by "educated" persons, that only an incorrigible absolutist will challenge their respectability.

As for Wilson Follett's parallel undertaking, *Modern American Usage* (published in 1966, three years after his death), the author's absolutist bias is everywhere apparent. In a chapter "On the Need of an Orderly Mind," he acknowledges that everyday usage often violates the "rules," but he still insists that the violations are "wrong." In most printed works, he remarks, "there will certainly be a good measure of standardized error that the orderly mind has

---

[9] One of the first was Porter G. Perrin in his *Index to English* (1939), later revised at intervals as *Writer's Guide and Index to English*. Another is L. M. Myers, whose *Guide to American English* (1955, with later revisions) is admirable for its frankness and good sense.

not even noticed." But if even the orderly mind does not notice it, how can it be called error? To the pragmatist, indeed (and I should think to any rational person), "standardized error" is a contradiction in terms. It is like talking about a "common rarity" or a "slight catastrophe."

So we must supplement the authorities by direct observation, taking note, in reading and listening, of each encounter with a supposed error; and when such encounters become routine, we may wisely decide that the change, though perhaps still offensive to *us*, is irreversible.

We may also listen to our own speech, if we can learn to do so without becoming painfully self-conscious, and if we are willing to be occasionally disconcerted by realizing, too late, that we ourselves have used a word or phrase that we would rather avoid. I judge that I myself, as a result of many years of teaching (and of controversy), am abnormally sensitive to what absolutists call errors, whether "standardized" or not. Yet I recently found myself saying, in conversation with an intimate and revered friend and former teacher (who does not share my pragmatic view of language), something like "between the chancellor and I." Such an occurrence can only mean that I have heard the expression (the use of "I" instead of "me" after a preposition or a verb, when a noun has intervened) so often, even in an almost exclusively academic community, that I have unconsciously accepted it. I shall still try to avoid what I still consciously regard as an error; but I have to assume that the error has now become "standardized"!

And in this case, what difference does it make? Unlike some usages previously mentioned, this one does not hurt the language. The meaning is clear; "I" is no less, or more, euphonious than "me"; if the usage offends, it does so because the hearer (occasionally) or the reader (more frequently) is in the habit of expecting "me." Why is such a habit worth fighting about?

Many of our language problems, indeed, arise from conflicting habits. Habit makes some words "unacceptable" simply because they are new, no matter how useful they may be; just as it eventually makes them "acceptable." "Maximize," for instance, sets my teeth on edge. It *sounds* unpleasant, to begin with; and it images a crude and bustling bureaucrat, a spokesman for big business or the military, talking of maximizing profits or the lethal power of a weapon; a person concerned with things and not with people, a would-be producer of a "bigger bang for a buck." Yet it aids communication, filling a void in the language. We were previously forced to say something like "increase to the highest possible point" or "to the greatest possible extent." Moreover, we have long accepted "minimize"—that it is not the opposite of "maximize" but means "to make *appear* less" is irrelevant—which may have been once as disturbing to untuned ears as "maximize" is to ours. (The latter was used, incidentally, by the famous English social philosopher Jeremy Bentham in 1802 and by the American philosopher William James in 1902.)

"Finalize" is another word whose novelty offends, but which is undeniably useful. We can of course be more specific, and *should* be, if the situation permits. We can say "sign" (an agreement), "approve" (plans), or "complete" (a tentative statement), if one of these is what is meant. But a general term is needed, and there is no reason why "finalize" should not be it, even though 90 per cent of the American Heritage Usage Panel disapprove.

Or take another object of absolutist anger, the use of "contact" as a verb, as when a salesman (the symbol of a pushing, profit-conscious society) tells a prospective client, "I'll contact you tomorrow." This is certainly easier and more economical than "get in touch with" or any alternative that I can think of. "Write" or "telephone" or "see" is not a substitute, since the medium of contact is as yet unknown. But somewhere, sometime—probably in a classroom or from a textbook when we were young—we got into the *habit* of thinking that "contact" as a verb is "wrong."

A particularly interesting example, where the absolutists support their dogma with some show of logic, is "center around." In geometry, the center of a figure is by definition a point, which obviously cannot be "around" anything, and the proper phrase *must* therefore be "center *on*." (If one were inclined to quibble, one might argue that since a point has no depth, breadth, or thickness—does not, in fact, have a material existence but is only an abstraction—nothing can be "on" it, and the proper word is "at.")

The fact is, however, that the argument is invalid. First, in a non-mathematical context, "center" does not always mean a point. When we say "the center of the city," we mean an *area*. Moreover, "center" is often used in a non-spatial sense; the "center" of a controversy may be a person, an abstract idea, a law, a policy, or almost anything. In these instances, a "center" may itself have a center, and "center around" makes perfectly good sense.

Even this argument, however, is irrelevant. Nothing matters except the fact that an overwhelming majority of people, whether "educated" or not, say and write "center around," and their hearers or readers know what they mean. Persons on both sides of the communications link have the same concept of something spreading out or gathering around, with reference to space or thought or action, something else of lesser magnitude; and for the life of me I cannot see why "center around" should not be used to convey this concept. At any rate, it *is* used. And therefore it is "right." (A related use is "round-pointed" shovels and "square-pointed" shovels. Must hardware stores rename these implements because, taken literally, the adjectives are nonsensical?)

To push the principle to its utmost imaginable limit, we may consider those not uncommon sources of horror or hilarity among teachers of "Freshman English"—the unconscious replacement of "take for granted" by "take for granite" and "would have" by "would of" ("I would of gone home"). It might be plausibly argued that the first usage is not unnatural, since "granite" suggests something that is hard, heavy, durable, something that guarantees a secure foundation; and it is an easy transition from the foundation of a building to the foundation of an argument. But again the only relevant question is not concerning the origin but only the use. If "take for granite" is ever accepted by a numerous public, it will have to be accepted by the dictionary makers. And the same is true of "would of," even though there is no possible way to rationalize its use. (The pronunciation, of course, is identical with that of "would have" in ordinary conversation.) I do not anticipate the acceptance, ever, of these expressions. But if it comes, so what?

We can perhaps clarify the principle further by noting how many everyday expressions are purely conventional and defy rational justification; are redundant, or self-contradictory, or divorced from the literal meaning of their components. Especially, we have the habit of sprinkling our speech and writing with unneeded "ups" and "downs." We "stand up" and "sit down," and waste a word in each instance. Similarly, we "fall down"—as if it were possible to "fall *up*"! We can, however, "climb down," a feat that off-hand would seem equally difficult. No more difficult, however, than to understand how a house can "burn up" and "burn down" at the same time; or how we can simultaneously "slow up" and "slow down" when we approach a stop sign or catch a glimpse of a police patrol car in our rear-view mirror. With a similar cheerful disregard of verbal niceties, we "shut up" or "shut down" a factory; or we watch a gunman in a TV Western "shoot down" a person while "shooting up" a town. All these expressions are justified by convention—that is, habit—and nothing more. We accept them because they are familiar; they are "right" because they are *used*.[10]

The importance of mere habit in the use of words leads naturally to the idea of "levels of usage," that is, the different habits in using language that people acquire through belonging to different social groups. A Harvard professor does not ordinarily talk like an assembly line worker for General Motors, nor does a Wall Street lawyer (not that Harvard professors or Wall Street lawyers are really much different from the rest of us) talk like a Mafia member, though in particular instances their basic values may not greatly differ.

Moreover, the same individual, if he is used to speaking in varying situations to different kinds of hearers, will as a matter of habit adapt his language to his audience. A scholar or scientist will use different language when speaking at a professional meeting in an auditorium full of fellow specialists than in gossiping with local colleagues during lunch at the Faculty Club. A supervisor in a factory will—especially if he desires to be promoted—use different language in reporting to a managerial superior than in giving orders to workers.

Similar distinctions are found in writing. An editorial writer for the *New York Times*, conscious of his paper's unique prestige and of its presumed obligation to guide the thinking of "educated" people, will word his analysis of a national problem differently than he would a personal note (possibly on the same problem) to a journalist friend.

---

[10] The supernumerary uses of "up" are almost endless; "rise up," "build up," "hurry up," "eat up" and "drink up," "finish up," "add up," "end up," "fix up," "pack up," "store up," "speak up," "write up," "sign up," "pay up," "buy up," "heap up," "slice up," "fry up," and so on and on. In the rural community where I grew up, it was customary to "bury up" a farm animal that had died of natural causes. All these are in addition to the many phrases in which "up" performs a real function. "Grow up," for instance, conveys the notion of a *completed* process.

These examples bring in question the definite distinction drawn by some authorities between spoken and written English, and the view that these constitute different levels of usage. It is true, of course, that there is some basis for the distinction. We write with the consciousness that words on paper receive more careful attention than words on the air. The reader must supply the emphasis and intonation that the spoken word carries automatically; and he can also pause at an unexpected word or phrase, whereas in listening he must keep up with the speaker at any cost, and has not time to be critical, except of extreme departures from what he feels to be the norm.

The reader of this essay will have noted, in fact, that some of the controversial expressions that have been discussed sound more natural in speech than in writing. Though possessed of "orderly minds," we might not notice such a "standardized error" as "The chairman invited Mr. Anderson and I to present our views" if it were spoken. In print, however, it might seem less standardized, and be noted objectively by the pragmatist and disapprovingly by the absolutist. In this connection, Mr. Bishop remarks concerning the *American Heritage* panelists: "Sixty-one per cent of them feel bad about the expression 'I feel badly' when they see it in writing; only 45 per cent object when they hear it in speech."

"Speech" here evidently means informal or conversational speech, for it seems clear that formal oral English, used in addressing large audiences (whether the text is prepared or extemporaneous), or in conferences or conversations where the participants are concerned only with impersonal matters, is identical with formal written English. On the other hand, a note or letter to a close friend, or even a frequent associate, would read exactly as an informal conversation would sound across a table at a coffee break or in the corner of a living room.

The real basis for distinguishing between levels of usage among educated people lies not in whether the utterance is written or spoken but in the relation between the persons involved. At one extreme there is in theory no personal involvement on either side; the communication is aimed at a general audience, at a group or a class or a whole society, perhaps even at a future audience yet unborn. The tie is a presumed common interest in what is being communicated, and there is a certain psychological distance between the speaker or writer and his audience that bars familiarity.

At the other extreme, there is a closeness—actual or assumed, physical or mental, friendly or hostile—between the user of words and the hearer or reader, which permits the former to put himself as well as his ideas into his utterance. He knows those whom he addresses, and he is either confident of their sympathy or willing to court their disfavor. He therefore uses shorter and more common words and does not calculate the effect of their sounds or associations. Contractions come naturally, slang needs no apology, unconsidered humor is in order. Instead of a judicious "It may be assumed," a statement may begin with a blunt "You've got to admit." Instead of saying (or writing) "It is difficult to discover the logic of Mr. X's argument," one may say (or write) simply, "X is an idiot."

And it is not only vocabulary that is different. Informal style is marked by relatively short loose sentences, the use of simile rather than metaphor, casual rhythms and stresses. In formal speech or writing, the sentences are more consciously shaped, by such devices as inversion and parallelism; metaphors probably outnumber similes, and the latter are more elaborate; the movement is measured by more pronounced rhythms and punctuated by sharper stresses.

I am speaking here, of course, of writing in which the author is either consciously or through habit seeking clarity and force. Many writers of utilitarian prose seem to respect neither their subject matter nor their prospective readers, using the words and sentence forms that first occur. (Not that every communication can or need be a literary masterpiece.)

Perhaps the most notable examples of formal English in conversation are to be found in Boswell's *Life of Johnson*. Goldsmith was justified in his remark that if Johnson "were to make little fishes talk, they would talk like whales." A disciplined mind and the habitual assumption of authority produced without apparent effort a measured and weighty utterance. Arguing against the authenticity of the *Poems of Ossian*, Johnson commented: "Supposing the Irish and Erse languages to be the same, which I do not believe, yet as there is no reason to suppose that the inhabitants of the Highlands and the Hebrides ever wrote their native language, it is not to be credited that a long poem was produced among them. If we had no evidence of the art of writing being practiced in one of the counties of England, we should not believe that a long poem was produced *there,* though in the neighboring counties, where the same language was spoken, the inhabitants could write."

No doubt conversation in the eighteenth century was conventionally more studied than at present, but Johnson in particular seems to have set himself a standard that forbade familiarity, and that sprang from a justified sense of his own ability. He had in his own eyes, as well as in the eyes of others, a character to live up to. "He seemed to take pleasure in speaking in his own style; for when he had carelessly missed it, he would repeat the thought translated into it. Talking of the comedy of *The Rehearsal,* he said, 'It has not wit enough to keep it sweet.' This was easy; he therefore caught himself, and pronounced a more round sentence: 'It has not vitality enough to preserve it from putrefaction.' "

Current taste no doubt finds the first phrasing admirable, the second intolerable save for the unintended humor. Even Johnson ran a risk in trying to maintain a consistent character; and it is delightful to find that on occasion he forgot to try. Roused at three o'clock in the morning by his young friends Beauclerk and Langton, he exclaimed: "What, is it you, you dogs! I'll have a frisk with you." On the other hand, even during his last illness, he told a physician who "hoped he was better": "No, Sir: you cannot conceive with what acceleration I advance toward death." We may smile at this, despite the occasion; and more broadly when we read his answer as to how he liked the person who had, in the absence of friends, "been employed to sit up with him": "Not at all, Sir: the fellow's an idiot; he is as awkward as a turnspit when first put into the wheel, and as sleepy as a dormouse."

In his letters Johnson lets down his guard still less often, and we are right in thinking of his style in terms of the famous rebuke to Lord Chesterfield. Yet in writing, too, feeling sometimes overcame habit, as in a letter to his friend Thomas Warton, who had been instrumental in his being awarded an M. A. from Oxford: "After I received my diploma, I wrote you a letter of thanks, with a letter to the Vice-Chancellor, and sent another to Mr. Wise; but I have heard from nobody since, and begin to think myself forgotten . . . Dear Mr. Warton, let me hear from you, and tell me something, I care not what, so I hear it but from you."

The point of these quotations (though one need never apologize for quoting Samuel Johnson) is that it is misleading to use such terms as "standard *written* English" and "colloquial [spoken] English." The levels of usage in question, which are certainly distinct, even though no sharp dividing line can be drawn, might better be labeled "formal English" and "informal English," either of which may be found in both writing and speech.

Even the absolutists would probably agree, at least in general, that formal and informal English should not be thought of as "right" and "wrong"; that the real question is, "What is *appropriate* in a given situation?" The trouble starts when the principle of appropriateness is applied to the language of different social groups—the "uneducated" and the "educated," "working people" and "professional people" (who of course do not work), those who say "ain't" and those who do not. What is appropriate in the home of a child belonging to the former class becomes "wrong" in the classroom presided over by a member of the latter. And without arguing, at this point, about the best solution to a difficult problem, we can surely agree that for such a child the experience cannot be other than painful and confusing.

It becomes still more so when racial tension is added; when a child finds that what he has always heard in a black ghetto is almost a different language than that which a white teacher from the suburbs tries to make him use. This is the extreme, and often tragic, form in which the problem presents itself; and in this form the problem is insoluble as long as we who follow a different verbal convention (and make the rules) insist that ours are "right" and those of uneducated blacks are "wrong." We must acknowledge that it is no more wrong for them to speak (and hence write, when they begin to write) as they have always heard those around them speak, than for Puerto Rican children to speak Spanish. It is simply a different way of using words. Since, however, it can be understood without much difficulty by anyone who knows English, it is assumed to be a deformed and illegitimate offspring of that language. On the contrary, it should be regarded, from a linguistic standpoint, as a perfectly respectable English dialect, with grammatical rules of its own, accepted and found adequate by those who use it.[11] It says with perfect clarity, and sometimes with force and

---

[11] The most obvious of these rules, or conventions, deal with the treatment of verbs—the omission of *s* from the third person singular present tense and the omission of *ed* from the past tense and the past participle. "He say he study the lesson" will be recognized by teachers who have known many black

beauty, what the users need and wish to say to each other, and therefore it is absurd to say that it is "wrong" when used within the group. To regard it with contempt or hostility is necessarily to indulge the same attitude toward those who use it. No sensitive teacher will ever try, from whatever motives, to make black students ashamed of their native dialect.

What such a teacher *will* do, at some point in their schooling, is place before students with a background of black culture the following proposition: *"If* you wish to enter the mainstream of American society, which is predominantly white; if you wish to compete successfully with white persons in business, or science, or the professions; if you wish to influence the forces that govern society, in order to lessen the injustices from which you—and other minorities—suffer; then you *must* learn to use English as it is used by the members of the group you wish to enter—the persons that you wish to compete with and influence. Otherwise you must be content with a job involving mostly manual or mechanical skills—not that there is anything demeaning in such work or that you should not choose it if you like it—unless you have rare natural gifts that will bring success in sports or in the arts."

Some black militants, and their white supporters, resent even this admonition. They argue that acceptance of it by a black student will mean the surrender of both his individual and cultural identity, and that what is called "success" by white middle-class society is at best unsatisfying and at worst corrupting. The linguistic goal for black students, they insist, is the mastery of their own dialect. "Bidialectism" is viewed as a formula for cultural suicide.

To this contention there are two answers, one based on a philosophical assumption, the other on stubborn facts. The first is a matter of faith—that "people are people," whether black or white or red or yellow, male or female, theist or atheist or agnostic, communist or capitalist in ideology, or otherwise distinguished by physical or intellectual, genetic or acquired characteristics; and that all human values ultimately inhere in the free and unique individual—even though these values can only be realized within a

---

students as a characteristic black formulation of what "standard" English would express by "He says (said) he studied (has *or* had studied) the lesson." The "standard" forms, it may be noted, are not essential to the meaning of the statement, since the time of the action would be clear from the context.

community, and self-fulfillment involves a measure of self-surrender.

If one dismisses such a faith as being "unrealistic" or makes the specious charge that it imposes on groups and individuals a faceless uniformity, it may still be defended as containing the only hope of saving the human race from self-destruction. For it is a matter of observation that conscious separatism, whether based on race, sex, nationality, ideology, or some other factor, either originates or results in an unfounded assumption of superiority, and hence gives rise to inevitable conflict.

In the case in point, we are all human beings, we are all Americans, we all have to live together, we all have to communicate with each other. And in personal [12] relations, the reasonable rule is to be ourselves, speak or write as we naturally would, and expect our associates to speak or write as *they* naturally would.

The second answer may be to many persons more compelling. The business of society—that is, the management of the production and distribution of goods and services, the sharing of information or theory among scholars and scientists, the shaping of policy in any group or community or organization—has to get done, and it can only be done if those who do it use a common language. Moreover, the common language must be "standard" English; not because it is necessarily a better instrument of communication than "black" English[13] or any other dialect (it probably *is*, since it has

---

[12] The term used in the social sciences is "interpersonal." What this adds to "personal" except five letters and a superficial impression of scientific exactness, I do not see—except, perhaps, in a particular context where "intergroup" relations might also be involved.

[13] This issue, the subject of bitter controversy, is irrelevant to the present argument. But I cannot resist inserting a quotation from a letter appended to a recent article in *College English* by J. Mitchell Morse, entitled "The Shuffling Speech of Slavery: Black English": "I doubt that the following paragraph from Marx's *Capital*, for example, can be translated into Black English. I know beyond question that people whose vocabulary and syntax are limited to those of Black English—or of Silent-Majority white English—cannot possibly understand it:

In proportion as exchange bursts its local bonds, the character of money attaches itself to commodities that are by nature fitted to perform the social function of a universal equivalent. These commodities are the precious metals. If money is to equate any other commodity to any amount, and thus to represent any exchange value that may be wished for, a material is needed whose every sample exhibits the same uniform

been developed through so many centuries and has been used by so many people, both in speech and writing, for so many purposes), but simply because it is the language that is used. As scholars, if they wish to enter the world of affairs, must speak the language of those who manage it, so must blacks use the language of the world they wish to enter. Every profession, every branch of the natural and social sciences, has its specialized vocabulary, and this vocabulary is invariably associated with standard forms and sentence patterns. One does not sacrifice his individuality by using such means of communication any more than a mathematician does by using a certain special set of symbols—or for that matter, any more than a newspaper reporter does by using a typewriter. "Standard" English is only a tool for performing certain functions, for achieving certain ends.

To be sure, not all blacks, any more than all whites, will wish to engage in work that is primarily intellectual, to say nothing of the life style that is generally assumed to go with it. And if they do not, they will never have to worry about standard English. But if they never have a *chance* to learn to use it, if white bigotry or black pride limits them to the dialect called "black English," the native talents of many will find no outlet. We may hold the opinion that some middle-class Americans are misguided in their choice of goals, but there is outside this class no imaginable future for black Americans who wish to work with their minds rather than their hands.

What has just been said about the social significance of "black English" for the people who use it is also true of the dialect used habitually by a great number, perhaps a majority, of white Americans, including many who, by economic standards at least, are indisputably middle class. Farmers, factory and construction workers, plumbers and truckers—those whose hands keep the wheels of a mechanized society turning—all speak a variety of English that is

---

qualities. On the other hand, since the difference between the magnitudes of value is purely quantitative, the money commodity must be divisible at will, and equally capable of being reunited. Gold and silver possess these qualities by nature." (XXXIV [1973], 841.)

What Mr. Morse's use of this quotation says about black English is problematical, but it clearly establishes his gift for unconscious humor. I ought to say, however, that the body of the essay contains a number of comments that *do* make sense.

called "illiterate" by those who make a point of not speaking it. And in school their children face a language problem similar to that of black children—including unimaginative and rule-ridden teachers. One hears in one's mind some dialog such as the following, interminably repeated.

"Johnnie, where's your arithmetic paper?"
"I ain't got none."
"You mean you don't have *any*. Say 'I don't have any.' "
"I don't have any."
"Why?"
"I di'n't know we was s'pose' to."
"*Were* supposed to, Johnnie."
"What?"
"Say 'I didn't know we *were* supposed to.' "
"I di'n't know we were s'pose' to."
"Didn't you hear me give the assignment yesterday?"
"I wa'n't here yest'y."

The way Johnnie uses English is the way millions of non-poor, non-black, perfectly respectable Americans also use it in everyday speech, and to call it "wrong" is simply to remove oneself from reality. This is the language—to strike a personal note—of the friends and neighbors in the small New England country town where I grew up—of my playmates, schoolmates, teammates in baseball (the passion of my young life!); and after almost half a century lived mostly in another world, I find it pleasant to be accepted still—by those still living—as one of them. They speak their kind of English and I speak mine, comfortably and unselfconsciously. The language, after all, belongs to them as much as to me.

But again, of course, there are contexts in which this kind of English is inappropriate. Persons belonging to the managerial or professional class have a different set of conventions in the use of language, and successful communication on their level demands that these conventions be adhered to. It is not necessarily snobbishness, therefore, nor loyalty to some linguistic ideal, that makes teachers try to force these conventions on uncomprehending children. They may be moved, rather, by the altruistic egalitarianism that we have been taught to value, in the abstract, as a peculiarly American virtue. This involves a faith, not consciously insincere, that every child, regardless of birth and background, has before him—or her—the possibility of "success," of what social scientists call, when the child's family has been poor and unlettered, "upward mobility."

It is not irrelevant, in an essay on language, to reflect for a moment on the use of this phrase. Perhaps few of the many people who pronounce it so casually ever think—though thinking is presumably what they get paid for—about what the adjective means. Does it mean making more money? But then are not construction workers better paid than many persons holding "white-collar" jobs? Does it mean that some vocations are intrinsically more desirable, or more honorable, than others? Or does it simply mean that more respect is paid in our society to those who belong to the managerial and professional class? And if the last explanation is correct, *are* these persons in fact granted greater respect by members of the "working class"? And if they are, *why* are they? And *should* they be? And again, why?

Why should a university professor, for instance, be looked up to by his students, except for his knowledge and the ability and desire to share it with his students? Or why—to raise a question that troubled me long before it was raised in dramatic form by the massive egotism of Richard Nixon and the reluctance of almost anyone outside the media to challenge publicly his pretension to absolute power—should the President of the United States receive, merely by virtue of his office, more respect than a garbage collector or a scrubwoman, if they do their job well and are decent human beings?

But though social status may often rest upon false values, and power be sometimes granted to those unworthy of it, the stubborn fact remains that place and power, even when sought from altruistic motives, are possible only to those who have some competence in using "standard" English. To impart this competence is clearly one of the things that schools are for. But how to actually move children or adolescents toward this goal, instead of creating confusion, shame, hostility, or apathy in those who lack a literary background, is a problem not easy to solve. The theoretical solution, perhaps, is bidialectism. But how exacly to apply the theory, how to get children to understand and accept a double standard in language, is still a problem. It is a problem, however, of which teachers of language at the elementary level ought at least to be aware.

The views presented in this chapter can be summarized briefly. In language, what is used is right—and *has* to be. There are no absolute "rights" and "wrongs," aside from the principle that whatever aids communication is right and whatever hinders it is wrong. Many traditional "rules" in textbooks and handbooks are contradicted by the way a majority of "educated" people actually speak and write.

This does not mean that "anything goes." Conventional patterns —levels of usage—exist in certain kinds of situations and among particular social groups. Among "educated" people, we meet both formal and informal English, both in speech and writing; and there are much more striking differences between the language, spoken or written, of this group of people and the language used by the perhaps larger group of "working" people (mostly spoken, since they have little need of writing). The language of the latter group cannot be called "wrong" (the phrase "levels of usage" does not imply that one level is absolutely "higher" or "lower" than another); but if a person who has been brought up to use it wishes to move to the other group, he must learn to use English as the members of that group use it.

3
GRAMMAR

The controversy over what constitutes "good English" abounds with references to "grammar." But probably not one in a thousand of those who spring so fiercely to the defense of this sacred entity has ever stopped to ask himself what it is, precisely, that he is defending. Quite literally, the self-appointed guardians of linguistic virginity do not know what they are talking about. One infers that what they have in mind is a set of rules that they once heard about in school, which are presumed to cover every aspect of communication by means of words, to which are attributed the perfect logic of Euclidian geometry (overlooking the fact that Euclid's axioms are only assumptions) and the universality of Newton's law of gravitation, with overtones of the Ten Commandments. "This," they seem to assert, "is what, by the laws of the universe, language *is*. And this is how we are commanded to use it, on pain of eternal damnation." That some people think of it and use it only as an instrument must, in the minds of these pious folk, be simply another manifestation of original sin.

One of America's clearest-sighted students of language, Paul Roberts, aptly observed, "If we knew what kind of English God speaks, we would have no problem, but we don't...." There are millions of Americans, however, who are not so modest. They know exactly how God speaks, and writes, English. They once read it in a high school textbook, or they were told in elementary school by Miss Smith. There is also, of course, the Bible—which of course they have never read. If its authors were divinely inspired, however, have its translators also received illumination from on high? We have in English many different versions, and if all are "the Word of God," then the Deity speaks English with even less consistency than most other users of the language.

No doubt definitions of "grammar" are as varied as translations of the Bible. In the widest sense it would perhaps be a complete description of how we communicate by means of words. But such a description seems impossible, since the meanings and functions of words are determined by the specific context, and the number of contexts is infinite. Even in dealing with a single language (for of course each separate language would have a grammar of its own), the efforts of grammarians can never have more than partial success, and in English at present there is not even agreement on the procedure to be followed. Within a generation we have seen traditional Latin-based grammar challenged by "structural linguistics," which in turn has been forced to give ground to "transformational grammar." Each system has been ingeniously elaborated and plausibly defended, and has doubtless contributed to the development of a genuine science of language.

The present essay, however, is concerned with practice and not with theory, with language as an instrument and not as an intellectual system. For the purpose of our discussion, then, I propose a very limited and very simple concept—that we think of "grammar" as merely the different *forms* of words that go with different *functions*. (The technical term for these different forms is "inflections." A highly inflected language, like Latin or Greek, is one which has many variants of a single root. Modern English and French, on the other hand, have relatively few inflections.)

We say "boy," for instance, when we mean one boy. (Women's Liberationists—with whose general aims I am in total sympathy—may mentally substitute "girl" for "boy." I refuse to say "person.") We add an *s* ("boys") when we mean more than one boy. If we wish to indicate that the boy or boys possess something, we add an apostrophe and *s* to "boy" and an apostrophe without the *s* to "boys": "the boy's books" (one boy), "the boys' books" (two boys or more). (In Anglo-Saxon, as I seem to recall from a course in graduate school, there are remnants of a "dual" number—a separate form indicating that exactly two persons or objects are being referred to.)

Next, when we say that one boy is doing something now, we add an *s* to the word that tells what the boy is doing: "The boy *looks* at the bird." When we refer to more boys than one, we leave off the *s*: "The boys *look* at the bird." When we refer to something that either one boy or more boys than one did at some time in the past, we add *ed*: "The boy(s) looked at the bird." And when we wish to indicate that a condition or action is continuing, we add *ing* (after inserting some form of the verb "to be" before the main verb): "The boy is (boys are) *looking* at the bird."

Again, when we use a word telling what the boy is like, such as "tall," and when we wish to compare him with another boy in this respect, we add *er*: "Tom is taller than Dick." Then, if Harry joins the other two, we change *er* to *est* and remark: "Tom is the tallest of the three." If, however, the descriptive word is such (for example, "athletic") that to add *er* or *est* would sound awkward, we indicate the same relationship by putting "more" or "most" in front of it.

Finally, if we wish to use a descriptive word to tell, not what something is like ("a desperate effort"), but how something is done ("he tried desperately"), it is seen that the second function is shown by adding *ly*. (There are, however, a few Anglo-Saxon words—such as "slow," "fast," "quick," "hard"—whch have always modified both nouns and verbs, telling *either* what something is like *or* how something is done, without changing their form. Not knowing this, some contemporary worriers about the language have been known to censure "Go slow" or "Come quick"—where a form in *ly* has developed—as corruptions. Of course, history is irrelevant here, and eventually the general rule may prevail—though "He ran fastly" or "He worked hardly" are a bit difficult to imagine—so that "Go slow" may pass out of use and may then be called "wrong." In the meantime, we may as well use the form that seems most[1] natural.)

These are the typical forms of four kinds of words, traditionally called "nouns," "verbs," "adjectives," and "adverbs," which comprise four of the traditional "parts of speech." They make up, along with the class of words called "pronouns," which are discussed below, the essentials of English grammar as defined for our present

---

[1] See the comment on "more" and "most" in the next chapter.

purpose.² These classes of words are sometimes called "content words." They are held together and placed in certain relationships with each other by the words traditionally called "prepositions" (such as "to" and "with") and "conjunctions" (such as "and" and "because"), which by themselves have no substance or meaning, give the mind nothing to work on. These are sometimes called "function words," and a complete grammar would have to take account of them, but since their forms never vary, they are not covered by our simplified definition, and may for the present be disregarded.

It is true that in practice the system just described involves additions and qualifications, and that some of these irregularities present real problems to users of the language. But the number and importance of these problems is ("are" would be formally "correct" but "is" sounds better to my ear) exaggerated by the public and by some teachers of English. To the ordinary person, concerned with language only as a means of communication, English grammar need be nothing to stand in awe of. It is simply a set of variant forms of words, which are, or presumably once were, useful in communication.

The class of words that varies most and hence most often causes difficulty is that known as "pronouns." But before dealing with these eccentric entities, we may observe that even the conformist class of words called nouns, whose forms were first described, are not without interest. (Nouns can be variously defined, but in a semipopular essay we may assume that almost everybody has some notion—and much the same notion—of what a noun is.) One surprising feature—surprising, that is, to those who think of grammatical patterns as universal, is how few forms there are: only four, compared to a possible dozen in Latin, not to mention the different "declensions." We could eliminate the possessive form if we followed the example of the French and said "the book of the boy(s)" instead of "the boy's (boys') book." And in fact we do follow this practice in the use of nouns attached to inanimate objects or abstract concepts, as in "the roof of a house" or "the root of an idea."

And we do not absolutely need different forms for the "singular"

---

² A strict application of the definition would perhaps include such items as the addition of *er* to a verb to form a related noun ("fight"—"fighter") or the addition of "like" to a noun to form a related adjective ("dream"—"dreamlike"). But these forms do not give rise to any practical difficulties.

GRAMMAR

(one) and the "plural" (more than one). Some English nouns do not have them; and not only a few names of animals from the Anglo-Saxon, such as "deer," "sheep," and "fish" (an alternative plural "fishes," used in the King James Version of the Bible, has now dropped out of use), but an abstract Latin term like "species." (Many persons who have not studied biology take this to be a plural form of which the singular is "specie"—which, however, has traditionally meant "coined money.")

Theoretically, then, an English noun need have only one form; and this is actually true of "species," since we never use a possessive form but say "a characteristic of the species" or sometimes, for convenience, "a species characteristic." (Many English nouns are used as adjectives—"cotton cloth," "animal tracks," "ocean currents"—without any change in form.) It is clear that in the use of English nouns, inflections are not essential to communication.

At the other extreme from the relative simplicity of nouns is the confusing multiplicity of pronoun forms. (Pronouns may for the present purpose be crudely defined in traditional textbook terms as "words standing for nouns.") Here, to limit ourselves only to "personal pronouns," there are twenty-five different forms. First, there are three "persons": the "first," the person speaking ("I"); the "second," the person spoken to ("you"); and the "third," the person or thing spoken of ("he," "she," "it"). Next, there are, in the third person singular, three "genders"—"masculine," "feminine," and "neuter"—whose forms have just been given. Also, there are, as in nouns, two numbers; corresponding to the singular forms given above are the plural forms "we," "you," "they." (In the third person plural, be it noted, there is only one form for all three genders.) There are, in addition, three "cases." One is the "nominative" (for which the English "subjective" might be better, although names do not really matter), denoting a person or thing that *is* or *does* something or has something *done to* it. ("*He* was wounded"; this statement is said to be in the "passive voice.") A second is the "objective" (in English, the Latin "dative" and "accusative" cases, referring to the use of a noun or pronoun as an "indirect object" or a "direct object," have the same form),[3] denoting a person or thing

---

[3] In "I gave him the book" the direct object (the thing given) is "book." The indirect object (the person to whom the thing is given) is "him." The relationships would perhaps be clearer if the statement (identical in content) were "I gave the book to him." "Him" may also, of course, be used as a

that something is *done to* ("The bomb wounded *him*"), or that forms part of a *relationship,* signified by a preposition such as "to" or "for," with something else ("The gift was for *him*"). The new forms here ("you" and "it" undergo no change) are "me," "him," "her," "us," "them." The third case is the "possessive," which has two groups of forms—one used with a noun and preceding it, as in "my (your, his, her, its, our, their) book"; and one used without a noun, as in "This is mine (yours, hers, ours, theirs)." ("His" and "its" are unchanged.)

This profusion of pronoun forms is of course quite needless; it is simply an unfortunate historical accident, which we now have to put up with. There is nothing inevitable, nothing consistent, nothing not purely conventional, about this system.

Let us, to begin with, take gender. Since it is indicated by three different forms in the third person singular, why not in the third person plural? Why not, that is, have separate forms to indicate that the *group* is exclusively masculine, exclusively feminine, or exclusively neuter? Why not, also, other forms to indicate that it is part masculine and part feminine, part masculine and part neuter, part feminine and part neuter, and, finally, part masculine, part feminine, and part neuter? And if in the third person, why not in the first and second? This fearful proliferation—some thirty forms before we even get out of the nominative case—is where a complete consistency would lead us if we were to infer from the third person singular that gender is necessary in communication in English.

Or, to put the question from the opposite point of view, "Since we get along without indication of gender in the first and second person singular—not telling whether the speaker (I) or the person spoken to (you) is masculine or feminine—and in all persons in the plural, why do we need it in the third person singular? The answer is that we do not need it; that we have it because we have it, just as we have toenails, which are not only useless but a nuisance. But there they are.

And if we continue to look at our list of pronouns, we find that other forms are also superfluous. In the second person, we have

---

direct object: "The dog's owner gave him to a friend." Hence, it makes no sense to talk about "dative" and "accusative" cases in English. The form is the same.

GRAMMAR

only one form ("you") for both the singular and plural numbers and for both the nominative and objective cases. Yet nobody complains that this causes difficulty in communication. So why should we not have a single form in the first person instead of four ("I," "me," "we," "us")? To this question no reasonable answer is possible. And if the question then is, "Why do we not have a single form?" the answer is, "We happen to be part of a society whose members speak English."

Further analysis of pronouns would only demonstrate more conclusively the absurdity of the whole system—*if* anybody insists on talking about "consistency" or "logic" or "law" in relation to grammar. So why not face the facts and acknowledge that language is what it is, and that words have different forms because they have them—that is, simply because the forms are *used*—and that if usage changes, language changes?

We observe this truth again in dealing with verbs, and, more specifically, we perceive the absurdity of trying, as absolutists in general have done, to construct an English grammar on a Latin foundation. "Regular" English verbs, as noted, have only four forms—the stem or root, used by itself or with the addition of *s, ed,* or *ing*. But what about Latin? First, there are three "persons"; second, there are two "numbers"; third, there are six "tenses" (present, imperfect, future, perfect, pluperfect, future perfect); fourth, there are three "moods" or "modes" (indicative, subjunctive, imperative—the last of which, however, we will omit from our arithmetic since it has a relatively small number of forms); and fifth, there are two "voices" (active and passive). If we multiply all these together, we get 144 different forms for each individual verb, not counting a large number of supplementary forms such as "infinitives," "participles," "gerunds," and "gerundives." That the functions of some of these forms are achieved in English by combining the *ed* form with some form of "have" or "be" only accentuates the difference between the two languages.

It is true that the system of English verbs is complicated by the persistence of several groups of Anglo-Saxon "strong" or "irregular" verbs, which usually have separate forms for the simple past tense and the past participle; forms which are typically derived not by the addition of a suffix (such as *ed*) but by a change in the stem vowel—for example, "sing," "sang," "sung." Somewhat more than a hundred of these are in common use, and since they follow a number of different patterns, historically explicable but apparently arbitrary, they cause some difficulty. Like the personal pronouns, they are historical accidents, which the natural genius of modern English—its tendency to simplify, to omit unneeded variant forms—has not been able to assimilate. A four-year-old child, following unreflectively the normal pattern of English verbs, will sometimes say, "I goed out" or "I hitted the ball," and even some of his elders may say "growed." But most of us learn by habit to accept the irregular forms that are used by most adults.

One group of irregular verbs, however, is even simpler than regular verbs, in that the "principal parts" are identical, and the only different form is the third person singular, present tense, which adds s. The significant fact for the present discussion is that these verbs, such as "hit" and "hurt," suffer no decline in usefulness or convenience because of the dearth of different forms.

What this analysis comes down to is that in English the function of a word is usually clear from its position and the context. Whereas in Latin, or other highly inflected languages, a writer or speaker might, as far as meaning was concerned, use words in almost any order, confident that the different endings would automatically assign each noun or pronoun to its proper verb in the proper way, and each adjective to its related noun, we find that in English, as a rule, a subject immediately precedes its verb and an adjective immediately precedes the noun it modifies. The meaning of "I hit him" would still be clear if the words were "I hit he" or "Me hit him" or "Me hit he"; it would always be clear who was doing the hitting (the person referred to by the pronoun preceding the verb) and who was getting hit (the person referred to by the pronoun that follows the verb). Moreover, the *time* of the action—whether it took place in the past, is taking place now, or will take place in the future—would be evident from what had gone before, and not from the form of the verb. Or if someone says, "Big Jack hit little Jill," we know who is big and who is little, as well as who was the aggressor and who the victim.

It follows that, because of the essential nature of modern English, many variant forms no longer have a function, but are simply inherited from a more highly inflected ancestral language. No doubt some forms are still useful, and a student interested in grammar for its own sake might wish to inquire which forms, exactly, need to be retained and which might in theory be discarded. But to

GRAMMAR

the pragmatist, such an inquiry is irrelevant. For him, the question is not whether the forms are useful but whether they are used. If so, they are correct, regardless of their history; if not, it is pointless to insist that they *should* be used.[4]

Readers can make their own applications of these ideas. The present work is not another "handbook" offering "easy-to-follow instructions" for unobservant and unreflective writers and speakers. (Not that handbooks are not valuable, if their point of view is pragmatic!) But brief comments may be appropriate concerning a few of the "rules" that have bedeviled generations of school children, college freshmen, and concerned adults.

We may as well begin with the mythical monster "Shall and Will," which is not less malign because its imagined lineage is illegitimate and its alleged usefulness is nonexistent. The rule that traditional textbooks have insisted on (first suggested by a seventeenth-century grammarian motivated by a natural desire for consistency) is in substance: "To express simple future time, use 'shall' in the first person and 'will' in the second and third; to express determination or promise, use 'will' in the first person and 'shall' in the second and third." The fact is that at no time in history and among the members of no social group has this rule been consistently applied. Even convinced absolutists, such as Wilson Follett in *Modern American Usage,* lose themselves in endless concessions, qualifications, and subjective judgments (in this instance through twenty-one pages), and I have no wish to be equally tedious in confuting them. But a few examples are in order.

One difficulty with the rule is that the distinction between expectation and determination is often impossible to draw. When Jesus says, in the King James Version, "Ask, and it shall be given you," is he making a promise or merely stating a fact? The second interpretation is suggested by the next verse: "For he that asketh, receiveth." Yet "shall" is used. And later in the same chapter of Luke, Jesus' hearers are told, "When the unclean spirit is gone out of a man, he walketh through dry places, seeking rest; and finding none, he saith, 'I will return unto my house whence I came out.'" This also seems to be a simple statement of intention, and again violates the rule. One would hesitate to assert that in the most famous En-

---

[4] To those who wish to read more on the subject, I recommend Otto Jesperson's *Growth and Structure of the English Language,* Chapter X, "Grammar." The whole work is excellent—scholarly, sensible, and readable.

glish translation of the Bible the use of "shall" and "will" is totally haphazard, but if there is indeed any governing principle, it is far too flexible and elusive to serve as any sort of practical guide. My own impression is that the choice is made, probably unconsciously, on purely rhetorical grounds: that "shall" *sounds* more emphatic and suggests greater intensity of feeling, and that the matter of "person" is largely irrelevant.

And this general principle seems to hold true both in other literary works and in current usage. When Hamlet answers his mother's plea, "Go not to Wittenberg" with "I shall in all my best obey you, mother," do his words convey a promise or a mere intention? The context makes them sound like a promise, yet "shall" is used. Or we may take a famous modern example, spoken on a historic occasion by a man distinguished for (among other things) his mastery of rhetoric: Douglas MacArthur's utterance when leaving the Philippines early in World War II. When the General said, "I shall return," he was certainly not making a simple factual statement about the future; he was expressing a fierce determination and making a sacred promise. One supposes that he knew the textbook rule but found it contradicted by his own conviction of the greater force of "shall."

As a matter of fact, "simple future time" is ordinarily expressed, in all persons, not by "shall" or "will" but by the present tense of "be" plus the present participle: "I am going to college next fall" or "When are you leaving the city?" or "She is coming on Sunday." Aside from forceful oral utterance, "shall" is now used naturally mainly in first person questions: "What shall I do now?" "Where shall we go?" Another common use, in legal documents and pronouncements, is purely conventional and is probably felt by most persons to be part of the unnatural language that helps to make the law incomprehensible to all but lawyers.

In recent years, however, I have occasionally encountered, especially in freshman compositions, the use of "shall" in the third person to express simple future time: "If the weather forecast is right, it shall rain tomorrow," How such a thing could come about is a mystery, unless through the half-successful efforts of English teachers to impose on passive and uncomprehending students the textbook rules concerning "shall" and "will." Whatever the origin, I feel, when I meet it, as if I had run into the edge of a door in the

GRAMMAR

dark. Nevertheless, it may eventually become respectable. In the annual report of the Foster Parents Plan for 1974 I read of "special 'teams' of case workers . . . who shall have special sessions with all Plan families." The context makes clear that there is no suggestion of compulsion, determination, or promise—nothing but a simple statement of intention. What is happening here, I do not know. But if it happens often enough, we shall get used to it (I see that I have used "shall" automatically but judge that most people would use "will"), and it will cease to be "wrong."

In the meantime, the only sensible answer to any question about "shall" and "will" is, "Forget it."

A similar case is that of "whom." It serves no purpose and causes endless confusion. If I were inclined to adopt an absolutist attitude, I would say: "Never use 'whom.' " Such questions as "Who did you give the book to?" or "Who did you see today?" register no discord in my mind, nor, I venture to think, in the minds of most other Americans. "Whom," on the other hand, *almost* always makes me uncomfortable. "To whom did you give the book?" is unthinkable in ordinary conversation. (There are always exceptions, of course; a person might be aiming at satiric emphasis, as in the rejoinder of a friend of mine whose husband casually remarked that he intended to have ten children. They already had four. "And whom," she inquired with what seemed innocent curiosity, "are you going to get to have them?") Only in the most formal written English could I use "whom" without a feeling of constraint. To be sure, it does have in the proper context a certain resonance that "who" has not. "For whom the bell tolls" is splendid rhetoric. (It was predictable that some critic of my pragmatic views would head his comment "For Who the Bell Tolls.") But it was used in a sermon more than three centuries ago.

And Donne's most famous contemporary, a popular playwright named Shakespeare, evidently shared my distaste for "whom" in everyday talk. Students of language will remember the scene where Hamlet, asked by Polonius, "What do you read, my lord?" answers for countless foiled and weary seekers for enlightenment, "Words, words, words." When the questioner, impervious to Hamlet's mood, persists in his question about the content of the book—"What is the matter, my lord?"—he receives the still more flippant answer, "With who?" Some may argue that Hamlet is being deliberately ungrammatical in order to underline his questioner's obtuseness. But in *Othello*, when Iago tells Cassio that Desdemona is married, the response is clearly unselfconscious: "To who?"

Oddly (as it must seem to those who hold that current indifference to grammatical niceties is proof that the English language is deteriorating), this particular usage—"who" immediately after a preposition—is one which most people today find upsetting; and as a rule, since they feel uncomfortable with "whom" under almost any circumstances, they avoid the construction altogether.

In another—perhaps the only other—situation where some of us hesitate to use "who," an alternative is fortunately available. Even a hater of "whom" will pause before saying "The man who I met" or "The woman who I talked to." The pronoun is so close to the verb or preposition of which it is so obviously the object, that our deeply implanted sense of *some* distinction between "who" and "whom" still acts upon us. In ordinary conversation most people would simply leave out the pronoun and say "The man I met" or "The woman I talked to." But if, in a particular context, clarity or emphasis demands that the pronoun be present, we can usually substitute "that": "The one person, and the only one, that I want to see punished is Blank."

But if in some situations we are able to evade or ignore the admonitions of absolutist teachers and texts, there are others where such admonitions have been less harmless, where the result has been confusion or inconsistency. One of these involves a clause beginning with "whoever" or "whomever," where the whole clause is used as a noun, the subject of a verb or the object of a verb or preposition, while the "correct" form of the pronoun is determined by its function *within* the clause: "You can give your name to whoever is in charge." Here the whole clause "Whoever is in charge" is the object of the preposition "to," and "whoever" is the subject of the verb "is." Or the noun clause can be the subject of a sentence: "Whomever you meet can give you directions." Here the subject of the main verb "can give" is the clause "whomever you meet," and "whomever" is the object of "meet."

Nobody not a slave to absolutist rules would ever use the last example. If happily ignorant, he would avoid it automatically; if aware of the "correct" construction, he would reject it as an intolerable affectation. In either case, he would probably use "whoever";

GRAMMAR

or perhaps he would say "anybody you meet." As for the first example, of course, it is natural as well as "correct." Unfortunately, some persons are haunted by the ghosts of prescriptions and proscriptions concerning "who" and "whom"; there are times, they seem to remember, when one is supposed to use the latter, on pain of being labeled "illiterate." What is unnatural, they have been made to feel, is nevertheless "correct." And so, whenever an adjacent verb or preposition makes the action plausible, they throw in a "whom" or "whomever": "Give the message to whomever is in charge." Of a similar kind is such a wording as (in a discussion of divorce in the Boston *Globe*) "failure to agree on whom should keep the children."

To uncorrupted minds, the governing principle in this area is that "who" (or "whoever") is the form that is *felt* to be appropriate at the beginning of a clause; position is more important than function. And since a relative (or interrogative) pronoun normally comes at the beginning, "who" is the form that is used naturally, and therefore properly, in all except a few situations.

One of these exceptions occurs where a short "parenthetical" clause intervenes between subject and verb, so that the pronoun at first seems to be related (as object) to the verb of the parenthetical clause, which is nearer, rather than to the more distant main verb of which it is actually the subject. "The chairman denied the vote to those *whom he asserted were not members*" or "He thanked the person *whom he thought had helped him.*" One need not, however, rely on hypothetical examples. Franklin Roosevelt, in the final speech of his most difficult campaign (a speech carefully prepared by the best speech-writing team that a Presidential candidate ever had), told his hearers that the question they should ask themselves was: "Whom do I think is best qualified?" And in a distinguished work of American literary scholarship, the editor slips into the same pattern and speaks of "writers whom he thinks should be included."

One would like to blame this usage, also, on the confusion once caused in students' minds by absolutist notions of grammar. But in fact it antedates even the founders of the absolutist faith. "Whom do men say that I am?" asks Jesus of his disciples in that unfailing source of linguistic heterodoxy, the King James Version of the Bible.

Of course, such "errors" do not really matter. They are probably noticed only by persons who are looking for them, and they never obscure the meaning. And since they occur so often, it would be wrong to call them "wrong." Still, in such mechanical matters, one is perhaps entitled to a prejudice in favor of uniformity.

This possibly tedious and too technical discussion may be lightened, in conclusion, by two real-life examples of something or other. One is a story told about her small daughter by a college faculty member, who, though generally committed to prescriptive grammar, possessed a sense of humor. One day she was baking or making something to give to a friend, and the little girl, whose name was Ursula, asked, "Who's that for?" Her mother corrected her by saying "Whom." Ursula, baffled, repeated, "Who?" and her mother patiently repeated the correction: " 'Whom, Ursula." At this point Ursula, determined to get to the root of the difficulty, demanded, "Well, who's Whom?"

The other instance is from a correspondent of Abigail Van Buren, which she printed (without comment) in her column: "Dear Abby: You can sure tell a lot about people by the way their children answer the telephone. We have taught ours to ask, 'Whom is calling, please?' " [5]

One hesitates even to mention "I" and "me." Though controversies once raged around these two small words, I suppose nobody not brought up on *Woolley's Handbook*, in the cave-dwelling past of English language teaching, ever says "It is I" or "Those are they." (The mind boggles—to coin a phrase—at the latter expres-

---

[5] In the *New York Times Magazine* of March 9, 1975, Theodore Bernstein has a light-hearted essay entitled "I Favor Whom's Doom." Only when it comes directly after a preposition would he approve its use. He proposes "that teachers of English drop the obviously futile attempt to implant into pupils' minds the senseless rules about *whom*." Of great interest is the result of his informal poll of twenty-five well-known writers, including some professional linguists. Fifteen agreed, six dissented, and four were "in-between." Among the dissenters was Russell Baker, who in his own column in the same periodical had earlier (October 13, 1974) made a plea for "whom" in the name of "elegance" and taken issue with Bernstein's position: "Give up the struggle with 'whom'? Come on, Bernstein, don't let the banner fall." Another "naysayer" was Lionel Trilling, on the ground that "confrontation" with the problem of when to use "whom" "tends to build character." (Can this be other than a tongue-in-cheek answer?) The big surprises, however, were among those who said "Yea": William Buckley, Jr. (no less), Jacques Barzun (one of the stoutest pillars of the traditional Establishment), and even Sheridan Baker! Perhaps the battle is over, and my own small arrow will only strike a corpse.

GRAMMAR

sion.) "It's me" and "That's them" have long since established their respectability in casual conversation. One only wishes it were possible to find an equally convenient formula for answering the opening query of a telephone call. "May I speak to Ms. Smith, please?" the caller asks. And Ms. Smith—if under fifty, say—will doubtless be sufficiently liberated from the trammels of traditional grammar to feel like a fool in answering, "This is she." Unfortunately, however, no acceptable alternative has yet appeared. If the call is serious, "That's me" seems too light minded. "Speaking," on the other hand, is so abrupt as to be almost rude. Yet it meets the test of clarity and economy, and an amiable intonation may forestall offense.

A more brilliant illustration than I myself can find or invent of the absurdity of the objection to "It's me" is offered by these delightful verses sent me by the author, Hughes Mearns. (They were originally printed in the *New Yorker* in 1947 under the title "Grammarian's Child.")

> When looking out I see a car
> Of friends come calling from afar,
> I cry to Mother right away,
> "Oh, that is they! Oh, that is they!"
>
> When in my room with girls and boys
> I hear, "Who's making all that noise?"
> I step outside and cheerfully
> Call down, "It's we! It's only we.' "
>
> When Teacher asks, "Who has, pray speak,
> A birthday in the coming week?"
> And *I* have, then I'm mighty spry
> To say, "Please, Ma'am, it will be I."
>
> But pounding on a bolted door
> With bears behind me, three or four,
> If I should hear, "Who *could* that be?"
> I'd scream, "It's me! It's me! It's me!"

It is curious that while the objective case ("me," "him," "her," "them") is replacing the nominative ("I," "he," "she," "they") after the verb "to be," a similarly "ungrammatical" change has been taking place in the opposite direction. As noted above in Chapter 2, many people (possibly a majority) now use "I" as the second member of a "compound object" of a verb or preposition: "The man in charge told John and I to come back later" or "She gave the money to Jane and I." Sometimes we even hear such a sentence as "Jane's friend invited her and I to dinner." And only the unobservant will be shocked to learn that I have regularly noted (more often, I think, in recent years) similar "errors" in the speech of colleagues in university English departments.

One may speculate, again, that this usage is due to an early infection of formal grammar and the resultant confusion. But in the Stratford Grammar School where Shakespeare was a pupil, it had not occurred to anybody that English grammar needed to be taught —only Latin. Yet the Bard has one of his heroes, Antonio in *The Merchant of Venice*, tell his friend Bassanio: "all debts are cleared between you and I." And this is not in light conversation, but in a letter written in the face of death.

So we find once more, as so often, that expressions currently denounced as illiteracies, and cited to prove the imminent decline and fall of the English language, have been for centuries in common and respected use. It is true, of course, as has already been stated more than once, that history is in one sense irrelevant, and that what is correct is what is current. But it *is* relevant in showing how unstable are the foundations on which absolutist rules are based, and how little we know of why—if it even makes sense to ask the question—particular changes in a language take place.[6]

The pragmatist, however, is concerned with results and not with causes. His question is simply, "How widely is this expression used, now? Is its use so common that, whatever our personal habits and prejudices, we may as well live with it?"

The list of what absolutists have labeled "errors," in defiance of usage, is long, and need not be pursued through increasingly trivial instances. But perhaps one more item may be mentioned, namely, the use of a plural verb or pronoun with a preceding pronoun that is singular in form but plural in meaning. Forty-odd years ago I insisted that students write, "Everybody should bring *his* book to

---

[6] Why, for instance, in the construction just discussed, does "I" occur so much more often than "he" ("between you and he"), while "she," "we," and "they" are almost never met with?

class." [7] Even then I was defending an anachronism—if indeed such a practice has *ever* been generally followed—and at present I venture the guess that nine-tenths of the population would say, "Everybody should bring *their* books" or "Everybody should support *their* President" or "Everybody has *their* own opinion." To take one of the countless actual examples that anyone may encounter, the late Bernard Baruch, millionaire "elder statesman" and adviser to several Presidents, observed in 1965 that "the important thing is the struggle everybody is engaged in to get better living conditions and they are not interested too much in the form of government."

Absolutists may find the last two examples especially offensive, since the singular verb and the plural pronoun, both related to "everybody," seem to clash. But, as so often in English, the form is unimportant. The eye registers "one" but the message to the mind is "more than one," and habit has accustomed us to ignore the apparent breach of logic, that is, of perfect consistency in applying a general rule. Here is an illustration of Emerson's famous statement: "A foolish consistency is the hobgoblin of little minds." And this sage remark is delightfully underlined in an illustration sent me by a friendly commentator on my notorious essay: "I saw that the house was on fire and that everybody was running out. I wondered if he all got out safe."

In the same general category are "nobody" and "none." The textbook rule is that the singular form of the subject demands a singular verb and a singular possessive pronoun: "None of the students *has* brought *his* book." But surely the rule is contradicted by actual usage. At a guess, nine out of ten people (including university English professors) use sentences like "Nobody remembered to bring their books" or "None of the students were prepared for the test." Of course, "nobody" and "none" by their very nature present an anomaly, and neither singular nor plural is logically appropriate. The words simply deny the existence of their antecedents.

---

[7] This was, of course, in the days before Women's Liberation had begun its justified assault on social attitudes and its largely unjustified assault on the English language, with its insistence on such absurdities as "chairperson" (which, however, we shall eventually get used to, if we must). Women's Liberationists ought to be grateful for the use of "their" described below, which saves them from insisting on the impossible "his or her"—or perhaps "her and his."

But behind the negative form of the words the mind grasps the notion of a group: "They—all of them—failed to remember to bring their books" or "They—all of them—were unprepared for the test." Once again, the form is distinct from the meaning, and the meaning naturally prevails.

The view of language presented in this chapter can be brought into focus by an analysis of what may be considered a classic statement of an opposing view. The author of the "Talk of the Town" in that Bible of American middlebrows, *The New Yorker* (stirred like many other persons by newspaper versions of my grammatical heresy) declared: "a school child should be taught grammar for the same reason that a medical student should study anatomy."

This analogy is false on two counts. First, it assumes that language can be anatomized with the same precision as the human body, that the elements of a sentence stand in the same fixed relation to each other as do the bones, muscles, glands, nerves, and other features of the physical organism. But the fact is that words are only symbols, and sentence patterns are only habits, and the possible variety of relationships is literally infinite. Moreover, a significant change in the structure of the human body occurs only during tens or hundreds of thousands of years, whereas significant changes in language may take place within the lifetime of a single person.

The second non-fact implied in the statement is that, just as a knowledge of anatomy is indispensable to the effective treatment of the body's ills, so a conscious knowledge of grammar is essential to effective speaking or writing. Any teacher of composition, however, has known students who could not label correctly a noun or verb, but who had no difficulty in putting them and the other "parts of speech" into accepted patterns, achieving clarity and sometimes felicity of expression. It has long been my considered opinion that the correlation between the ability to analyze a sentence—to take it apart according to the principles of traditional grammar—and the ability to put a sentence together so as to satisfy the traditional demands of good taste and good sense, is zero.

This subjective judgment is supported by a study sponsored by the National Council of Teachers of English, published in 1963, entitled *Research in Written Composition*. After surveying the published research on how students acquire writing skill, the authors found that no positive conclusions were possible, but that one negative conclusion could be "stated in strong and unqualified terms: the teaching of formal grammar has a negligible or, because it usually displaces some instruction and practice in actual composition, even a harmful effect on the improvement of writing."

The same unconsidered bias that underlies the *New Yorker* statement is expressed even more bluntly by J. Mitchell Morse in the essay on "Black English" referred to above: "A person who has difficulty with the agreement of subject and verb can't think clearly." Since he gives no examples (one of the elementary requirements of clear exposition), the mental process by which he arrives at this conclusion remains obscure. It is hard to see the connection between thinking clearly, on the one hand, and, on the other, knowing whether "is" or "are," in a given situation, is preferred by a majority of the members of a particular social group. "They's all crooks" may not be fully accurate as an assessment of the character of federal government officials, though it may be natural to a black dweller in the District of Columbia; but the question of whether it expresses "clear thinking" has no discernible connection with the coupling of a singular verb and a plural subject. The meaning of an English sentence is determined by the position and specific content of *all* its elements, not by the author's choice among a few variant forms.

This is not to say that a writer or speaker, if he wishes his ideas to be accepted, can ignore the verbal taste and habits of his audience. In fact (as the reader may now be tired of being told), it is precisely this taste and these habits that, in a particular situation, make a particular usage "right" or "wrong." Only, a person must not let himself be bullied into believing that all the paths to verbal power have been charted and fixed forever, and that he must follow them in submissive obedience to commandments carved in stone.

4
CHANGE

Just as many absolutists have never thought about the nature of grammar, so they have never considered the fact of language change. Language is something that is used by living people, whose ways of life and thought are never static; and the verbal forms and patterns that are expressive of these changing ways must also change. This process has been continuous since human beings began speaking; it will end only when they cease speaking. The only languages that do not change are those that are no longer spoken and are properly called "dead."

Of course the experience of those who used them still lives. The agonies of Oedipus will still hold readers in awe when the Freudian theory attached to his name has become only a footnote to the history of psychology. But no one will ever again present a "criticism of life" in classic Greek. And Virgil's account of the meeting in Hades between the penitent Aeneas and the unforgiving Dido is a deathless illustration of the "tears of things" from which human life will be forever inseparable. But Latin, too, though it survived as the language of learning in Europe for a thousand years after the military and political fall of Rome, no longer records the thoughts and passions of living persons. Even the Roman Catholic Church, the great repository in the Western world of ancient forms and creeds, has lately recognized this fact by permitting the liturgy to be performed in the native language of the persons who participate; and Pope Paul is said to have written his first encyclical in his native Italian, after which it was translated into Latin by Vatican scholars.

CHANGE

Yet in a sense Latin is still alive—in Italian, French, Spanish, and other modern European languages derived from it by the process of linguistic change that has just been referred to. And presumably few people would now wish that these changes had not occurred. Yet such a wish would be no more at odds with reality than the apparent desire of countless contemporary Americans to curb the wayward tendencies of the English language and lock it safely within the walls of tradition—a tradition, moreover, conceived of as having been far more confining than the reality was. To them, change is synonymous with corruption; any significant, and sometimes insignificant, alteration in the verbal habits of society is a symptom of degeneracy, an omen of decline and fall.

It is, of course, a human trait to wish to perpetuate familiar things, to shrink from what is new and strange, to suffer pain in parting from the past. Yet on the other hand, we recognize that change is a condition of what we know as "life." And beyond this, there is also rooted in us some quality that permits us, at least sometimes, to see change not as a threat but as a challenge, not as the death of something but as the birth of something.

It is safe to say, nevertheless, that in the Middle Ages the few who were literate deplored the corruption of Latin in the speech of the many who were not—if indeed they thought it mattered how the masses spoke. Yet such an attitude is understandable in the light of their linguistic ignorance and their faith in a God-centered universe, in which change was perceived as a falling away from perfection, caused, like the original Fall, by human sin. It was a bold and visionary act of Dante, even at the beginning of the Renaissance, to write his masterpiece in the "vulgar" tongue. But that there should be today among educated people a widely shared and vehement opposition to language change as such, is hard to understand. Even editors and English teachers, who ought to know better, seem often to share this psychological bias, along with many non-literary people who perhaps should not be expected to know better, but who might be expected to be less assured in parading their prejudice and less obstinate in refusing to be enlightened.

For the fact is that to talk at any time about a language as if it were perfect, and as if any change must be for the worse, is to talk nonsense. It is true that particular changes may be judged to be good or bad, according to whether they are thought to make the language a more effective or a less effective instrument of communication. Some of my own regrets and biases have already been recorded—the loss of "disinterested" in its traditional sense is one example—in the chapter on "Usage," and others will be noted below. But language change in itself, taken as a whole, is neither good nor bad. In fact, it is pointless even to raise the question. One might as well ask whether sex is good or bad, or whether it is good or bad that salt and sugar taste the way they do. These things simply *are*. They are facts of life.

In this context we may consider the statement of an editorial writer for one of Boston's leading newspapers, under the heading "English or Choctaw." (What does he have against Choctaw?) After praising "vernacular" as "the growing edge of the language," he continues: "Under this tissue is, has to be, the skeletal structure of classic form which has been centuries in growing. Ours in English is at least 3000 years old, or older."

For the informed and thoughtful reader, the first fact that leaps out of this statement—typical in its general drift of the beliefs of an undoubted majority of Americans who have attended school— is the writer's ignorance of the history of the English language. What exactly he means by "the skeletal structure of classic form," it is impossible to guess. But concerning the age of the language, the truth is that Modern English is at most 500 years old. (In the nature of things no hard and fast line can be drawn between "Modern English" and "Middle English," which was the language of Chaucer.) Of the many languages whose contributions to it can be more or less clearly charted, two were dominant: Anglo-Saxon and Norman-French. The event that led in time to their amalgamation, the Norman Conquest, occurred about 900 years ago. Each of these languages was in turn the result of earlier amalgamations which can now be only imperfectly traced. And if we go back 3000 years, we go back to a time when the languages of Western Europe were not yet being written. Scholars can draw some inferences as to what they were like, but only two things about them are certain: first, none of them was the direct ancestor of Modern English; and second, each of them was itself the product of continuous change, from a beginning of which nothing can be known.

The editorial writer again reveals how ill-considered are his opinions when he talks about language "growing." A language may "grow," to be sure, by increasing the number of words that it contains, as English is now doing at a terrifying rate. But it does not

CHANGE

"grow" in the sense of moving from a less perfect to a more perfect state, nor in the sense of passing from infancy to maturity. A language at any time presumably meets the needs of the people who use it.

Moreover, if the "skeletal structure" of the English language has been "growing"—that is, changing—why should anyone suppose that it has stopped changing, or that it ought to stop? The apparent answer has already been suggested: that the physical law of inertia that governs bodies of matter ("a property of matter by which it remains at rest or in uniform motion in the same straight line unless acted upon by some external force") has a psychological counterpart in human beings; that they would like to continue exactly as they are and to have their world to do the same.

All this is so obvious that one hardly knows what more to say. Yet the storm of protest that greeted *Webster's Third New International Dictionary*, partly directed at the editors' outright recognition of the fact of linguistic change, was a powerful illustration of the general lack of enlightenment. Perhaps a few examples will help dispel this intellectual darkness.

The two literary landmarks by which many adversaries of change direct their course through the menacing jungle of modern usage, and to which they turn their faces in worship like Moslems toward Mecca, are the works of Shakespeare and the King James Version of the Bible. But does anyone now speak or write the language of these masterpieces, though this language is classified as "Modern English"? Would the Supreme Court decision against prayer in the public schools have been more palatable to some professed Christians who attacked it if it had been put into the language that is used in the King James Version to express a similar prohibition on the part of Jesus? "But thou, when thou prayest, enter into thy closet, and when thou hast shut the door, pray to thy Father which is in secret; and thy Father which seeth in secret shall reward thee openly. But when ye pray, do not use vain repetitions, as the heathen do; for they think they shall be heard for their much speaking. Be not ye therefore like unto them; for your Father knoweth what things ye have need of, before ye ask him."

It needs no scholar to point out the changes that have taken place. We do not now use "thou" and "thee" for the nominative and objective cases of the second personal singular pronoun, nor do we use "ye" for the nominative plural; all these forms have been replaced by "you," as "thy" has been replaced by "your." And we do not end the second person singular verb in the present tense with *est* or *st*, nor the third person singular with *eth* or *th*. Absolutists will also be pained by the use of "shall" in the third person to express (as I interpret the passage) "simple future time," and perhaps by the phrase "have need of," which ends with a preposition.

The language of the King James Version was somewhat antiquated, even in its own day, based as it was in part on earlier translations; and it is hard to find in Shakespeare, a popular dramatist writing plays in up-to-the-minute idiom, so many archaic grammatical forms in a single passage. Yet he frequently distinguishes the second person singular from the plural, both pronoun and verb. "Thou canst not say I did it," cries Macbeth to the ghost of Banquo, "never shake / Thy gory locks at me." And the *th* ending in the third person singular remains in "doth" and "hath" for "does" and "has," although elsewhere the *s* ending regularly prevails. The envious Cassius exclaims of Caesar, "Why, man, he does bestride the narrow world / Like a Colossus. . . ."

The abandonment of these forms in later years might be plausibly deplored. To my ear, "thou canst not" has far more force and spirit than "you cannot," and "does" and "has" similarly deprive the language of part of its former grace and make it flat and pedestrian. Nevertheless, "thou canst" is now as dead as the divine right of kings, and "doth" and "hath" have likewise felt the killing touch of time. Even the most ardent defender of tradition would not attempt to resurrect them.

The vocabulary of the Elizabethan Age is even more at variance with twentieth-century usage than is the grammar. In the Gospel passage on prayer, we would not now use "which" in referring to a person, nor "like unto" in a comparison. Though "much speaking" is terse and vigorous, one would have to mark it "unidiomatic" if it appeared in a freshman composition. "Closet," moreover, no longer means "a monarch's or official's private chamber for counsel or devotions," but a small windowless room for storing clothes.

As for Shakespeare, he can now be fully understood by ordinary readers only with the aid of a glossary and notes. What can we make of Hamlet's "By heaven, I'll make a ghost of him that lets me!" as he breaks away from Marcellus' and Horatio's restraining hands to follow his father's ghost—unless we know that "let" means here not "permit" but almost its opposite, namely, "hinder" or "hold back"? (The old usage survives in the phrase "without let or hindrance.") Or how can we interpret Shakespeare's apology in Sonnet 76 for the lack of variety in his verse:

Why write I still all one, ever the same,
And keep invention in a noted weed. . . ?

unless we know that "weed" means, not a plant that one wants to get rid of, but a garment (as in "widow's weeds"); "noted," not "famous" but "familiar"; and "invention," a process concerned not with mechanics but with imagination?

Any casual reader of Shakespeare can extend the list, pointing out (to add a few random examples) that "fool" is often a term of endearment, while "fond" means "foolish"; that "honest" means "chaste" and "luxury" means "lust"; that "censure" means merely judgment or opinion, not necessarily unfavorable, and "knave" means "boy" or "servant," with no suggestion or rascality; that, on the other hand, our morally neutral "practice" means "treachery" or "conspiracy," and that "ecstasy," our word for indescribable joy, means "madness."

Has the language of Shakespeare therefore been corrupted? Or has it perhaps been improved? Are the changes good or bad? Almost everybody would agree, I assume, that these questions make no sense; that a language at any time in history is simply what it is, and that words are used as they are used; that Shakespearean English is one thing and twentieth-century English is another.

But when it is suggested that there have been changes between 1925 and 1975 which seem on the way to becoming established with equal firmness, and which it is equally futile to condemn, the outcry (as shown at the beginning of this essay) is swift and strident.

To be sure, as the reader is now aware, some usages that are supposed by many persons to be new, and that are attacked as corruptions, are in fact as old at least as the Age of Elizabeth I. On the other hand, in the forty-odd years since I began teaching college English, there have been, unless my memory fails me or I was then less sensitive, significant changes in both grammar and vocabulary. Those persons who contend that the language is deteriorating are half right; the changes that they deplore have certainly taken place. Where they are wrong is in the value judgment that the changes are necessarily bad.

When we study the grammatical changes, we see that most of them are in line with the natural tendency of English toward simplification, toward the abandonment of useless—though also, occasionally, of useful—forms. One instance of the latter—the banishment of a form that had real functional value—is what has happened to the verb "might." In form, this is the past tense of "may"; but the very meaning of "may" precludes a past tense, and "might" in actual use has implied a conditional state of things, in which it is possible that something *could* be done (in the future) or *could* have been done (in the past) *if* a certain condition is or had been met: "John might go to the meeting if he should feel well enough" or "Jane might have gone if she had felt well enough." [1]

What has happened is simply that "might" is no longer used by younger writers; in all cases it has been replaced by "may." These persons would naturally write (and of course say), "John may go to the meeting if he feels well enough" or "Jane may have gone to the meeting if she felt well enough."

In regard to the possible future action, it seems that little has been lost. As far as the literal meaning goes, I see no difference between "he may go" and "he might go." The only distinction is one of suggestion or feeling. "Might" seems to accentuate the uncertainty, to hint that a mental state is involved as well as a physical condition, whereas "may" is more matter-of-fact. But at best the distinction is tenuous, and I am disinclined to challenge the tacit judgment that it is not worth preserving.

But the case is different when past action is referred to. "Jane may have gone" means, or used to mean, that the speaker *does not know* whether she went or not, whereas "Jane might have gone" meant that she did *not* go, although it was possible for her to do so, or would have been possible under certain conditions. Now, however, "may" is the form that is regularly used, and the reader is forced to guess whether she went or did not go. It seems to me

---

[1] The verb in the conditional clause in the first sentence might (the unreflective use of "might" reveals my age) have a variety of forms: "should feel," "were to feel," or simply "feels." This situation shows our current uncertainty about the use of the subjunctive mood, which is discussed below.

that the absence of precision is a loss to the language, and I wish it had not occurred. But it *has*.

After all, however, this situation does not arise so frequently as to present a serious problem. More often the change occurs in a slightly different context. Once one would have said something like "Last year he said he might go to college in the fall"; now the statement would be "Last year he said he may go to college in the fall" (of last year). If this outrages older readers, I have to confess that it also jars me a little. At the same time, I call their attention to a statement by Senator Edward Kennedy in response to a Boston *Globe* "Spotlight Team" investigating Chappaquiddick. There was a question as to the origin of the party preceding the tragedy, and the Senator explained that at an earlier gathering "there was some suggestion that at sometime during the summer they may come up to the Cape." A similar use occurred in a recent CBS broadcast (February 3, 1975) concerning Watergate, where a speaker remarked that John Dean "decided to tell the truth and let it fall where it may." (The speaker must have had vaguely in mind the time-worn admonition to "hew to the line and let the chips fall where they may.") And on a Bill Moyers program (March 20, 1975) an authority on conservation observed concerning a worker's preference for a job, when jobs and conservation seemed to conflict, "If we were that man, we may feel the same."

If I were younger, I might (may) myself be using "may" in such statements. But at this point the conscious effort involved in such a change seems scarcely justified.[2]

[2] To support my position, I offer the following additional examples of "may" where "might" would once have seemed appropriate. The Boston *Globe* (February 13, 1975) quoted David Bartley, Speaker of the Massachusetts House of Representatives, as saying of his relations with Governor Dukakis: "It may be a desirable thing from a good government point of view if we didn't get along." And in Benjamin Bradlee's recent book about President John F. Kennedy we find the following: "The President noted that what he called 'Jackie's guilt feelings' [about her trip aboard Onassis' yacht] may work to his own advantage" by leading her to accompany him to Dallas. Of course, in some of these instances it may be the reporter who is responsible for "may" and not the person to whom it is attributed. But in either case the illustration is valid. And then there is the professional defender of capital punishment who concluded that between 1933 and 1969 "an additional execution per year... may have resulted on average, in seven or eight fewer murders." Though in substance the statement is wildly speculative, the language, specifically the use of "may," is unquestionably conventional.

Meticulous readers may have paused (perhaps they did and perhaps they did not!) at one of the illustrations above—"Jane may have gone to the meeting if she felt well enough"—not only because "may" is used instead of "might," but because in the subordinate clause they expected the verb to be "had felt" instead of simply "felt." The expectation is natural in older readers; I myself share it, and mentally grope for the missing "had." But it is gone, probably forever, and future generations will not miss it. I make this judgment not merely on the basis of many compositions by college students but on constant encounters in the press. In a story on Boston's controversial Park Plaza development a *Globe* reporter writes: "The head of the $2 billion real estate division of the Connecticut General Life Insurance Co. said he would not have expressed interest in providing $30 million backing for Park Plaza in 1971 if he knew then what he knows today." Can the head of a $2 billion operation be wrong?

In all situations, in fact, "had" plus the past participle (labeled in textbooks the "pluperfect" or "past perfect" tense and described as referring to a time preceding another time in the past) has now been replaced by the simple past tense. People do not now say, "After he had finished the job, he went home" but "After he finished the job...."

The same change has occurred in conditional constructions. Most college students with whose writing I have been familiar, and whose language habits reflect those of the middle class to which they belong, would not say or write, "If I had studied more, I would have got a higher grade" but simply "if I studied more...." Or the statement might be, "I would have studied more if I *knew* the exam would be so hard." They seem to have no feeling that "had" serves any purpose, and this feeling seems to be general.

In this connection, there are even some signs that the "present perfect" tense ("have" or "has" plus the past participle, referring to an action performed or a condition existing at some time preceding the present) is also yielding to the simplifying tendency of the language. A news story in the Boston *Globe* about the alleged sugar shortage of 1974 refers to "the United Fruit Company, which owned Revere [Sugar Company] since 1914." And in another story we read, "Mitchell . . . served on the council since 1965" (and still does). Indicative of the same trend are such questions as "Did you do it yet?" (rather than "Have you done it yet?") and such statements as "I did it already."

Well, why not? Anglo-Saxon got along with only two tenses, past and present, and so can Modern English. What difference does it make in the preceding sentences whether "have" or "has" is used or is omitted?

Another grammatical form that has vanished from some contexts where it was formerly used is the "comparative degree" of adjectives, which has given way to the "superlative." Except when it immediately precedes "than" (expressed or implied), the form ending in er is being ousted by that ending in *est*. Even when we are talking about only two routes to a given destination, we normally ask, "Which is the shortest?" And concerning two brands of the same product, we inquire, "Which is the cheapest?" ("Which is shorter?" and "Which is cheaper?" would be more economical, and to me they *sound* better. But most people do not use them.)

And this trend is not confined to the unlettered. The average English professor, if asked to compare the charms of two candidates for some kind of campus queen, would undoubtedly reply (if this was what he thought), "Janie has the cutest face, but Jeanie has the nicest curves." Or on a more academic topic he might inquire of a colleague, "Which of these two texts do you think is the best?" To which the answer might be something like "X has the fullest explanations, but Y has the clearest illustrations."

The "comparative" and "superlative" forms of adjectives presumably go back to a "dual number" in Anglo-Saxon. But an absolute ban on the *est* form in comparing only two things is said to have been decreed for the first time in the eighteenth century by a grammarian named Lowth, who, like many of his contemporaries, believed that the use of language should be ordered with the same consistency that was attributed to the other operations of a clockwork universe. We, less inclined to accept such unstudied assumptions, feel no guilt when we use an *est* form to compare two things. In general, either form is acceptable; the meaning is clear from the context, and the speaker or writer should use whichever form seems more natural. (To me, here, "more natural" is more natural than "most natural.")

An appropriate conclusion to this analysis is the ancient anecdote (evidently invented by some Harvard-hater) about a Harvard-Yale football game, which Harvard won. The Yale men took their defeat like gentlemen, and sent a congratulatory telegram to their opponents: "The best team won." The Harvard men acknowledged the tribute in an answering telegram: "The better team won."

A final item in this incomplete catalog of grammatical changes that are currently in process concerns the "subjunctive mood" of verbs. In the group of languages to which English belongs, it apparently developed as a means of referring to a condition that does not now exist or an action that has not yet taken place, but that may exist or take place in the future, and that is the object of a wish or hope, a doubt or fear, a command or request, or a mere supposition. And such a supposition may apply not merely to the future, but to something that is, or was, contrary to existing fact.

Unlike some related languages, such as Latin and Anglo-Saxon, Modern English has no distinct subjunctive forms. The functions served in other languages by separate forms are assigned in English to forms that already have functions of their own. These include: the simple infinitive ("The officer ordered him *to go*"); "may" or "will" preceding the infinitive ("I fear he *may* [*will*] die"), or "might"—until recently—or "would" ("I wished I *might* go" or "I hoped he *would* go"); in the third person singular, the same form (the s omitted) that is used elsewhere in the present tense ("The officer demanded that the robber *surrender*"); "be" in all persons instead of "am," "is," "are" ("I insist that I *be* released" or "He has asked that you *be* present" or "It is necessary that he *be* told the truth"). In the last two instances, to be sure, although the form is not unique, it is not what we expect following the particular subject, and yet we feel that it is needed. We would not say (although sometime our descendants may), "I insist that I *am* released" or "He has asked that you *are* present" or "It is necessary that he *is* told the truth." (Somehow the last of these does not sound so bad.)

Yet in these latter instances, though the subjunctive forms are needed, we seem not to be quite comfortable when using them. We try to avoid them by such phrasings as "I insist *on being* released" or "It is necessary *to tell* him the truth." Or we try to disguise them by inserting "should" ("The officer demanded that the robber should surrender" or "He has asked that you should be present"). Or sometimes we simply discard them and use the "indicative"— especially after "if." We no longer say, as some of our ancestors did, "If he *be* guilty" or "If the story *be* true" [3] but "If he *is* guilty" or "If the story *is* true."

Even the "contrary-to-fact subjunctive" about which the absolutists are adamant ("If he *were* guilty, he would not have surrendered" or "If the story *were* true, it would not have been denied") is giving way to the indicative ("If he *was* guilty..." or "If the story *was* true..."). To be sure, the meaning might (there it is again!) be different; whereas "were" says that he is *not* guilty, that the story is *not* true, "was" seems to offer an alternative: perhaps he *was* guilty, perhaps the story *was* true. But the context usually tells us what is meant.[4]

So it appears that as the language changes, the subjunctive mood is gradually being eliminated as a distinct system of verb forms. The functions for which these forms were once felt to be necessary are now carried out, for the most part, by the same words that serve more common functions. And another set of "rules" can be in large part forgotten.

The changes in grammatical forms, which may have less interest for the general reader than for the student of language, are less obvious and dramatic than changes in the meaning of words. The former take place gradually, and the feelings that produce them are often vague; but the latter may occur with relative suddenness, and the new meanings are often in conflict with the old. To use a biological analogy, the former are the result of a sort of natural selection, while the latter are more like mutations.

---

[3] Noah Webster, in the 1828 edition of his *Dictionary*, says the use of "be" in such constructions "was in a great measure discarded before the time of Addison" (i.e., before 1700).

[4] Occasionally we find writers using "were" where "was" is not only the form that most people would use but the form that most of the "experts" would judge to be "correct." A news story on the Middle East reports as follows a statement by Secretary of State Kissinger: "that as long as he *were* involved, the United States would never tamper with the basic security of Israel." (Presumably his words were "as long as I am involved," and the "were" is the reporter's.) Perhaps a more significant instance is found in an interview with Igor Stravinsky, in which the composer is quoted as saying, "I should feel I *were* betraying music if...." Doubtless in his native tongue the subjunctive would be natural in this situation, which is hypothetical and not factual. But ears attuned to Modern English respond as to a false note in music.

The list of examples that might be given is long, and I remind readers once again that this essay is not intended to supply a comprehensive guide but only to state and illustrate a principle, and to make people aware of the challenge that change presents; of the need to make their own judgments, however modest and tentative.

Already, in the opening chapters, there have been discussions that would be appropriate here; for instance, of "disinterested" and "uninterested," "infer" and "imply," "flaunt" and "flout." In each of these pairs the same process has been taking place: the first word loses its original meaning and appropriates the meaning of the second, which then passes out of use. The process in these instances is not complete, but the pace is accelerating, and a reversal is unlikely. We may deplore these particular changes, as I do, but we have no reason to think that the forces by which they are decreed will be responsive to individual resentments or regrets.

An identical case is that of "convince" and "persuade." It is true that the confusion here is of long standing. Writers of textbooks for at least fifty years—since I was a college freshman—have been trying to convince their readers that "convince" involves purely *mental* acceptance, presumably based on logic or evidence, of the truth of some assertion; and to persuade their readers to use "persuade" only when conviction is followed by *action*. It is possible that these efforts had some temporary effect, but of late it has become increasingly clear that absolutism has lost the battle. In the *New York Times Book Review* of October 27, 1974, two different reviewers innocently used "convince" with reference to action. One spoke of "the economic incentives and imperatives which convince a writer to move on before he has really developed his theme." The other, regretting that "business biography is such a neglected area of study," remarked: "I guess the trick is to convince someone to spend several years writing the life of such an egregious bore" as John Wanamaker. How is it possible—and why should anyone try—to make the general public preserve distinctions of which professional writers are unaware?[5]

Or consider "verbal" and "oral." The latter once meant "spoken," whereas the former referred to *any* communication by means of

---

[5] Noah Webster gives "persuade" as a synonym of "convince," and gives as one definition of "persuade," "to convince by argument." He seems to make no distinction between *conviction* and *action*.

words, whether spoken or written. But at present "verbal" invariably means "unwritten," and "oral" in the sense of "spoken" is now rare in popular usage. (The younger generation probably associates it mainly with discussions of sexual behavior!)

Other apparent changes are perhaps too recent for a final judgment. One of these involves "repel" and "repulse." I have always thought of the latter as referring to physical force, the former as usually applying to states of mind. I am *repelled* (I would have said) by the absolutist view of language; and I *repel* the suggestion that my view is antisocial. "Repulse," on the other hand, I am willing to leave to reporters of robberies, rapes, and wars. But I find that college students nowadays (I do not remember that it was so during my earlier years of teaching) are invariably *repulsed* by things they do not like (such as required courses and competitive grades). And I find a professor of English writing of a certain poet that "at Harvard he was repulsed by the obsequiousness of 'men who never knew me.'" (Perhaps my impression is a personal one, which systematic research would not sustain.)

Even harder to get used to is what seems to be happening to "incredulous" and "incredible." The former has hitherto described the *person* confronted with some assertion that he finds it impossible to believe; it has been the *assertion* that was "incredible." Yet in many people's minds today, it seems, "incredulous" applies not to the unbeliever but to the unbelievable. Thus, an opponent of abortion, attacking an advocate of it, writes in a letter to the editor in the Boston *Globe*: "it apparently seems incredulous to her that Pope Paul could seriously say that abortion is never permissible." And a *Globe* reporter, in the story on Chappaquiddick referred to above, says of a certain statement by a witness at the inquest: "the judge found that incredulous." Since I do not suppose that readers of and writers for the *Globe* are less literate than the rest of the population (even when they are anti-abortionists or Kennedy detractors), I conclude that here we may have the beginning of a change in the meaning of a word.[6]

---

[6] The dates of these quotations are, respectively, November and December, 1974. Neither Wilson Follett in *Modern American Usage* nor the editors of the *American Heritage Dictionary* take note of this new meaning of "incredulous." *Webster's Third* labels it "obsolete." This is surprising until one turns to the *Oxford English Dictionary*, which gives five examples of "incredulous" in the sense of "unbelievable," including one from Shakespeare and

All these instances involve pairs of related words. But of course single words are also subject to changes in meaning. "Decimate," for example, once had a specific, limited application—to the punishment of a Roman military unit, for some breach of the established code, by the execution of every tenth man, chosen by lot. This particular product of the military mentality is no longer customary, but the feeling seems to have remained that so forceful a word should be preserved, and it came to be applied to any extraordinary loss of lives by an army in battle. The next step was to generalize the application to make it signify the infliction of a severe injury or loss of any kind. And now we find it often used as meaning merely "to cause to deteriorate." A 1974 CBS broadcast on Cambodia spoke of the conflict in that tortured country as "decimating the quality of life." And the writer of a recent letter to the Amherst (Mass.) *Record* protested that a proposed road "would decimate one of the few tracts of open land near the town's center."

By this time the reader may feel that I have more than made my point about the frequency and inevitability of change in the meanings of words. Yet a student of language finds such changes endlessly fascinating, and I yield to the temptation to afflict the reader ("afflict" and "inflict" are two more words with a tendency to exchange identities) with two more examples. One is "enormity." I have always been impressed with the word's power to suggest a monstrous degree of *moral* obliquity. "The enormity of Nixon's conduct" is a phrase that I would have delighted to savor if his actions (that is, the worst of them) had occurred a generation ago. But now it appears that the moral freightage of the term has gone overboard; the word has become synonymous with, and has replaced, "enormousness." Its present connotation is purely quantitative.

Hence, in an *Audubon* magazine article on wind power, we are told that "there is no disputing the enormity of the kinetic energy resource in the global atmosphere." And the Boston *Globe* editorializes: "He is aware of the enormity of the task." (I have forgotten who "he" is, as well as the nature of his "task.") Similarly, a *New York Times* article speaks of "the enormity of the trade possibili-

---

one from Sir Thomas Browne. It also gives four examples of "incredible" meaning "unbelieving"—one as late as 1761. Let absolutists beware of "the whirligig of time."

CHANGE

ties." And in the *Times Book Review*, the chairman of the Department of Economics at Princeton writes of "the enormity of the difficulties that exist." [7]

So, if I am to indulge my fondness for "enormity" in the old sense, I shall have to turn to the literature of the past. I shall also have to find some other epithet for Nixonian behavior. Perhaps "heinousness" will do.

The second additional example of a word's changed meaning is one—the only one, I think—that I profoundly and intensely resent. The word is "gay," and it could once be used to designate one of the most cherished and endearing of human traits. It portrayed a person who was lighthearted but not insensitive, laughter-loving but never unkind, zestful but not aggressive, graceful in movement and gracious in mood. Now it means "homosexual." Of course I agree that people have a right to their personal sexual preferences, and am glad to see the old stigma removed, the old abhorrence overcome. But I do not agree that they have a right to deprive lovers of language, and lovers of friends without regard to sex or sexual attraction, of one of the most enchanting words in the English language. But in the realm of language, of course, there are no rights of any kind; there are only realities.

It may be an anticlimax—or perhaps only a renewed invitation to boredom—to make brief mention of changes in spelling and pronunciation. Compared with the changes in word meanings and grammatical forms, they are relatively non-controversial. In this area most people seem willing to either agree or else agree to disagree. Yet it may be relevant to remark that these changes occur with as casual disregard of historical antecedents as do other kinds of language change.

One change which is somewhat controversial involves nouns from Greek and Latin whose singular form ends in *on* (Greek) or *um* (Latin) and whose plural ends in *a*. Absolutists would have us retain the original forms and functions, but usage has ruled otherwise. Since almost nobody now studies Greek or Latin, most users take the plural form, since it has no *s*, as being singular. Then, if a need is felt for a plural form, an *s* is added to the original plural. How many persons know, or stop to remember if they once knew,

---

[7] Ninety-three per cent of the *American Heritage* Usage Panel find "enormity" in this sense "unacceptable." Too bad.

that "criteria" is strictly a plural noun (from Greek) with a singlar "criterion"; or that such words as "data," "strata," and "media," historically, are Latin plurals whose singular forms are "datum," "stratum," and "medium"?

Of these words (there are some others of the same kind), "criterion" rarely occurs in ordinary usage; the regular singular is "criteria" (a *New York Times* story speaks of Consolidated Edison as "the largest privately owned electric-gas utility by nearly every criteria"), which at the same time continues to serve as the plural. "Datum" is used still more rarely, and "data" is so clearly standard as the singular ("the data is . . .) that no examples are necessary.[8] As for a new plural form, which would be "datas," it seems not to be needed. Oddly, I *have* encountered "stratas" (a *Globe* columnist discussing the social effect of the rising cost of higher education speaks of "sheepskin stratas based often only on the ability to pay dormitory costs"), although "stratum" still occurs, and "strata" is often recognized as plural. As for "media" (popularly used mostly in referring to the "news media"), its widespread use is so recent that no particular pattern has yet become standardized. Eventually, however, like other Latin plurals ending in *a*, it will almost certainly be treated as singular. In the meantime, we need not fear that failure to use the classic forms will limit our "upward mobility"; the forms that we naturally use will be those that we have usually heard and read, and these will be the forms that *other* people have heard and read and accepted.

An especially instructive instance of how and why spelling changes occur, involves the name of the flower that gardeners usually refer to collectively as "glads." The scientific name of the genus to which it belongs is the Latin *Gladiolus* (because the leaves are shaped like swords), and this is also its name among non-scientists. But of course it is singular, and a plural is necessary. When a person says, "A bouquet of ———," what *does* he say? "Glads" will do in an informal situation, but (like "cops" for police officers, which is not normally derisive or hostile but simply neutral and therefore not offensive) there are some occasions when it is scarcely suitable. The Latin plural is "gladioli," but few gardeners are Latinists and, as just shown, Latin plurals have not had a high survival

---

[8] It is acceptable to 50 per cent of the *American Heritage* Usage Panel.

CHANGE

rate in English. "Gladioli" does not seem to be an exception. On the other hand, the Anglicized plural "gladioluses" is obviously unusable.

The solution chosen by the Burpee Seed Company (and perhaps others, since my research on the topic has been less than exhaustive) is simply to treat the singular form as plural: "Burpee's famous gladiolus *are* attractive and admired in the garden...." There is no reason why this should not be acceptable, if it is accepted. But one may guess that most people, when they pronounce the word, have the mental picture "gladiolas" (singular "gladiola"); and recently I encountered this in print. In an article in *International Wildlife* the author speaks of "carnations, lilies, gladiolas, and roses." We shall have to wait and see which spelling eventually triumphs. Predictions are as perilous in linguistics as in economics, but I would bet on "gladiolas."

For a final comment on language change, we can do no better than go back once more to Samuel Johnson. He compels our admiration, despite his Tory bias, by the firmness of his grasp on reality, and, despite his constitutional melancholia, by his ultimate trust in life.

Like the absolutists of our own day, he sees the language as being "exposed to the corruptions of ignorance and the caprices of innovation." It is with evident reluctance that he confesses, in regard to spelling, "I have been often obliged to sacrifice uniformity to custom." And he will surrender no more than he has to: "tongues, like governments, have a natural tendency to degeneration; we have long preserved our constitution, let us make some struggles for our language."

Yet unlike many Tories, past and present, he refuses to indulge in self-delusion. "When we see men grow old and die at a certain time one after another, from century to century, we laugh at the elixir that promises to prolong life to a thousand years; and with equal justice may the lexicographer be derided, who being able to produce no example of a nation that *has* preserved *their* words and phrases [emphasis added] from mutability, shall imagine that his dictionary can embalm his language, and secure it from corruption and decay, that it is in his power to change sublunary nature, and clear the world at once from folly, vanity, and affectation.

"With this hope, however, academies have been instituted, to guard the avenues of their languages, to retain fugitives, and repulse intruders; but their vigilance and activity have hitherto been vain; sounds are too volatile and subtile for legal restraints; to enchain syllables, and to lash the wind, are equally the undertakings of pride, unwilling to measure its desires by its strength."

Yet his final attitude is not one of merely stoical acceptance, but rather of measured rejoicing. Even if his dictionary *could* "embalm his language," even if his authority *could* prevail, this would not be his wish. "If an academy should be established for the cultivation of our stile," it would be a project "which I, who can never hope to see dependence multiplied, hope the spirit of *English* liberty [emphasis in the original] will hinder or destroy...."

I join in the tribute of Thomas Carlyle: "Brave old Samuel!"

TWO — STYLE

5
CLARITY

In the debate between absolutists and pragmatists, a common tactic of the former is to remark (with quiet triumph in being able, as they think, to remove the mask of objectivity from the face of snobbishness): "We notice that *you* follow the rules, even though you condemn them; language that you say is good enough for other people is apparently not good enough for *you*." The criticism would be legitimate—one ought to practice what he preaches—if it were relevant. But it misses the point of the pragmatist position: that good writing, or speaking, is not the result of following rules, whether prescriptive or permissive, but of exercising individual choice; not a matter of law but a matter of taste; not a matter of right or wrong but of relative success or failure in the always imperfect process of sharing experience by means of words.

The pragmatist in language would minimize the clash between older forms and newer ones. He would have the upholders of what they contend is traditional ask themselves whether their hostility to what they view as a graceless innovation is due to anything more than habit—whether in truth there is some intrinsic objection to the usage. He would have people recognize that language is what it is— something that they can neither change nor prevent from changing, but something that is given them to *use*. And he would ask them to agree that the only issue is how each individual can fashion from it the instrument best suited to his purpose.

What we are talking about now is *style*. And this is what the present work is, finally, all about. The analyses of "usage," "grammar," and "change," though justified in themselves as an effort to show what the English language is like and how it works in the everyday world, were a prelude to the more difficult and perilous endeavor to suggest how the language *ought* to be used. It is not enough to clear away the ancient walls and barbed-wire fences, the "Do Not Enter" and "Trespassing Forbidden" signs that have made the road to success in writing so dreary and unadventurous that many who have set out hopefully upon it have turned back, frustrated and disheartened. A fortunate few will find their way unaided across the rugged landscape, but most will need some compass bearings and landmarks, some understanding of the stages of their quest.

To be sure, this landscape has already been surveyed and charted many times, both by writers of textbooks and by those who have themselves been masters of style. But many persons have found that their textbook maps were inadequate, or that later, when needed, they have faded from memory; and they have never found their way to where the works of the masters repose unread on library shelves. Moreover, the landscape changes as the years pass —not in its basic conformation but in its outward guise. Old trails are abandoned and overgrown, and new ones are opened to new generations of travelers. And the earnest searcher will also find that every guide has had his own favorite routes and resting places, that one will recommend this safe and well-trodden way along the valleys, and another, that rough and lonely but far-vistaed track across the heights. So it may be hoped that one more overview will not be out of place.

The need exists especially for those who seek to master the written word (including formal speeches which are written and then read). Most people can make themselves understood, after a fashion, when talking face to face. The hearer can ask questions, the speaker can repeat, explain, illustrate. Sentences are punctuated by gesture and intonation. But a writer must succeed at once, with one specific arrangement of a single set of words. If he fails at first, he gets no second chance.

It is therefore evident that the first and greatest virtue of prose style is clarity. It is like "charity" in the King James Version of Paul's First Epistle to the Corinthians. Writing that does not have it "profiteth nothing." Though the writer may have "the gift of prophecy, and understand all mysteries, and all knowledge," these gifts are nothing to his readers unless he can find the words and fashion the sentences to make them clear.

We are assuming here that the writer is honest, that his aim is enlightenment and not deception. When a military command refers to a planned bombing raid as a "protective reaction," or a press secretary describes a Presidential statement as "inoperative" when in fact it was false, what we are faced with is not a legitimate use of words but their perversion and prostitution. Whether the verbal skill involved in plausible deception is the same as that by which honest persons convey what they see as truth, is a question that I would rather not get into; though I should like to think that language in its essence is a unifying and creative, not a divisive and destructive force, and that falsehood is *ultimately* (emphasis must be added) self-defeating. At any rate, the present essay is unlikely to be used as a manual of public relations.

Clarity, of course, is relative to the subject matter. Simple facts about the physical world, which (we assume) we all perceive in essentially the same way, can be conveyed with relative accuracy in simple words and simple sentences. But the workings of the mind, the swirls and surges of fear and hope, of rage and remorse, of desire and delusion, which are hardly to be spoken of as "facts" because we have so little certainty as to how far our own experience corresponds to that of others—are harder for language to seize and hold and pass on to an audience. Words must be chosen not only with a knowledge of their overt, explicit meaning, but also with a guessed-at notion of their associations, however misty and remote; positive assertions must constantly be qualified, in sentences of increasing complexity; metaphor and analogy must constantly be invoked—the author must be forever falling back upon "as if. . . ." In this context, the effort to achieve clarity is endlessly demanding and always destined to only partial success. We have, in fact, not even any certain means of measuring the degree of our achievement. Yet the effort must continue.

It is true that this kind of writing occurs more often in works of fiction than in the communications of everyday existence, whose functions are usually to inform, to influence opinion, or to move to action. Yet even in common life there are numberless situations in which the outcome is determined by whether the thoughts and feelings of the persons involved, their attitudes and purposes, are clearly communicated to one another. In political elections, in many court procedures, in social adjustments, in personal relations above all, facts are often less important than feelings, and the ability to express the latter is crucial to a fair and firm conclusion.

Still, perhaps it is in the representation of imagined experience that we can most easily find forceful illustrations of the different kinds of language that are called for in clearly presenting the experiences of the senses and of the mind, reality in its objective and its subjective phases.

By a lucky accident, the two most noted American novelists of the twentieth century are mainly concerned, respectively, with the kinds of experience, and hence use the kinds of language, that I have tried to describe. No novelist, of course, can ignore the inner life of his characters. Yet in the work of Ernest Hemingway our sharpest memories are of sensuous experiences—primarily visual, though also at times involving hearing and smell and taste and touch. The picture of the running of the bulls in *The Sun Also Rises* is unforgettable.

> There were so many people running ahead of the bulls that the mass thickened and slowed up going through the gate into the ring, and as the bulls passed, galloping together, heavy, muddy-sided, horns swinging, one shot ahead, caught a man in the running crowd in the back and lifted him into the air. Both the man's arms were by his sides, his head went back as the horn went in, and the bull lifted him and then dropped him. The bull picked another man running in front, but the man disappeared into the crowd, and the crowd was through the gate and into the ring with the bulls behind them. The red door of the ring went shut, the crowd on the outside balconies of the bull-ring were pressing through to the inside, there was a shout, then another shout.
>
> The man who had been gored lay face down in the trampled mud. People climbed over the fence, and I could not see the man because the crowd was so thick around him. From inside the ring came the shouts. . . .

William Faulkner, also, can appeal powerfully to the senses, but what engages him most fully is the challenge to express the inward life of human beings at the moment of most passionate stress. Though like Hemingway he is often preoccupied with death, his concern in the following scene from *Light in August* is with the

CLARITY

onlookers' perception of what is in the departing consciousness of the obscenely murdered man.

But the man on the floor had not moved. He just lay there, with his eyes open and empty of everything save consciousness, and with something, a shadow, about his mouth. For a long moment he looked up at them with peaceful and unfathomable and unbearable eyes. Then his face, body, all, seemed to collapse, to fall in upon itself, and from out the slashed garments about his hips and loins the pent black blood seemed to rush like a released breath. It seemed to rush out of his pale body like the rise of sparks from a rising rocket; upon that black blast the man seemed to rise soaring into their memories forever and ever. They are not to lose it, whatever peaceful valleys, beside whatever placid and reassuring streams of old age, in the mirroring faces of whatever children they will contemplate old disasters and newer hopes. It will be there, musing, quiet, steadfast, not fading and not particularly beautiful, but of itself alone serene, of itself alone triumphant. Again from the town, deadened a little by the walls, the scream of the siren mounted toward its unbelievable crescendo, passing out of the realm of hearing.

There will be little disagreement about the excellence of the passage from Hemingway, or its relevance to a discussion of clarity. But about the Faulkner there will surely be violently conflicting judgments. Some persons may dismiss it as a gross example of sophomoric over-writing. To others it may seem (leaving out the physical details) a sort of sonorous incantation, the words equivalent to notes of music, to which the question of clarity of intellectual content is patently irrelevant. Others will take it on what they consider to be the author's intended terms as an effort to etch upon the reader's consciousness an image corresponding to a supersensuous but distinct and powerful experience. To the accusation of lack of clarity they would reply that it lies not in the inadequacy of these words, but of *any* words, to the task imposed upon them— and imposed legitimately, in view of the author's purpose.

But whatever the simplicity or the complexity of the subject matter, the first requirement of clarity is the choice of the exact word. Even in describing physical existence, one is faced with many choices. If a teacher asks students in class to suggest words expressive of different ways of "going" (the general term) under one's own power from one place to another, the number of possibilities turns out to be astonishing. Someone says "walk"; then comes the realization that there are many ways of walking, and a torrent of suggestions is let loose: "stalk," "stagger," "swagger," "march," "stride," "pace," "saunter," "loiter," "plod," "trudge," "stumble," "tramp," "tiptoe," "trip," "amble," "ramble," "straggle," "limp," "hobble." . . . "Run" offers almost as rich a variety of words that have a visual impact: "race," "sprint," "dash," "gallop," "jog," "trot," "rush," "lope," "lumber," "scamper," "skip," "skitter," "streak," "flee," "chase." . . . Miscellaneous means of locomotion include "crawl," "creep," "scramble," "clamber," "leap," "hop," "wriggle," "slither," "steal," "dance," "totter." . . .[1]

Or if one were to ask for words descriptive of different *moods*, one might get "happy" and its many variants: "ecstatic," "joyful," "delighted," "contented," "cheerful," "sunny," "pleasant," "glad," "merry," "blithe" . . . ; "sad" and its verbal relatives: "mournful," "melancholy," "sorrowful," "downcast," "depressed," "dejected" . . . ; another family group including "grim," "gloomy," "somber," "sullen" . . . ; and a list of somewhat similar terms carrying a threat of aggression: "hostile," "angry," "furious," "fierce," "savage," "wrathful." . . .

It is fun to play the game of synonyms. Young writers sometimes buy a thesaurus and revel in the riches that it offers. What they have yet to discover is that no two words have precisely the same meaning, and that the practical value of a book of synonyms lies mainly in saving time for a writer who already understands the distinctions but cannot on the instant call to mind the uniquely appropriate term. It has even been suggested that the whole of *style* is finding the one right word for any given context, and if one had to accept a simple definition, perhaps this would be it.

But what is "right"? Are there any general principles according to which one may decide that some kinds of words are more right than others (to adapt George Orwell's famous phrase)? In fact, there *are* such principles. And one of them, particularly relevant to clarity, is that, other things being equal (of course, they never are!),

---

[1] Readers who want to play this game again might think of ways of *speaking*.

those words are best which are short, simple, plain. The most permissive teacher of composition will in this instance (if he understands his art) acknowledge the need for an absolute rule: "Never use a big word when a little one will do."

Some young writers will chafe under such a restriction. And, indeed, the tendency to resort to a polysyllabic vocabulary is not usually the fault of the user. His high school teachers may have encouraged him to indulge in resounding words and flowery phrases; perhaps because *their* teachers had never impressed upon *them* the virtue of simplicity. I recall that when I was a senior in high school I had such an English teacher—a pretty, friendly girl just out of college, whom I liked and wished to please. There was one occasion, however, when we disagreed. It was the custom at graduation, rather than inviting some locally prominent person or some professor from a nearby college to be the speaker, to select four members of the graduating class to address the audience of families and friends. Of course the speeches were carefully written out, under the guidance of the teacher of "Senior English," and memorized. I was one of the four, and my proposed beginning sentence was: "Tonight the class of 1924 must say goodby to Arms Academy." This struck my English teacher as too plain and commonplace for so momentous an occasion. (Dr. Johnson would have agreed with her that "this was too easy.") She suggested tactfully that it would be better to begin with some more impressive phrasing such as "On this memorable evening of June 24" instead of "Tonight." In fact, she felt that the style of the whole essay, which was in keeping with the opening sentence, needed to be made more elegant. I naturally assumed that she was right, and made a genuine effort to follow her advice. In the end, however, I had to confess that I could not do it—that what I had to say had to be said my way. Being a modest person, she did not press me.

Of course, I was right. And I have often wondered, since, how I unconsciously acquired this perception that the simplest way of saying things is usually the best. Or perhaps it is natural, and its rarity among writers of published prose results from the corrupting influence of their verbal environment. The fraternity of social scientists in particular are notorious for their use of language that is familiar only to their fellow initiates, and that the mere "intelligent layman" may question the need of. Witness the following passage from *Coping* by Daniel Moynihan—who, one would think, since he has chosen to enter public life, would wish to be understood by at least the more literate part of the public: "I accept fully ... the Weberian analysis of E. K. Francis that the ethnic collectivity represents an attempt on the part of men to keep alive on their pilgrimage from Gemeinschaft to Gesellschaft ... some of the diffuse, ascriptive, particularistic modes of behavior that were common to their past."

This is no way for an honest Irishman to talk. Perhaps the reader pauses longest at the three adjectives modifying "modes of behavior." "Diffuse" and "particularistic" seem, if I understand them at all, to contradict each other, and "ascriptive" is not to be found in either the *American Heritage Dictionary* or *Webster's Collegiate.* (That it is presumably derived from "ascribe" does not help.) One wonders, in fact, assuming that for a sociologist these words *do* have meanings in this context, whether those meanings add anything essential to the main thought or whether they might simply be omitted; whether the writer is indulging, from mere habit, in professional jargon—which is, moreover, superfluous.

Going back to the beginning of the sentence, one supposes that a scholar's conscience leads Mr. Moynihan to mention E. K. Francis as the source of the "analysis" that he refers to. But why burden the sentence (and the reader) with a reference to Weber? To those who are familiar with Weber's theories, it is needless; to others, it is meaningless.

Next, as to "ethnic collectivity," we all have some notion of the meaning of "ethnic" (which perhaps is used so much because it is so useful), but with "collectivity" we draw a blank—unless "ethnic collectivity" means the same thing as "modes of behavior ... common to their past." But if so, we are being led in a circle: "X represents an effort to keep X alive."

Finally, "Gemeinschaft" and "Gesellschaft" may, for readers who are fluent in German, have shadings of meaning that are missing in "community" and "society." But if a person is writing in English, does he not in resorting to foreign terms short-change his readers? Is he not guilty of (in current slang) a cop-out?

In plain English, the quoted statement might read: "I agree with E. K. Francis that when an ethnic group becomes part of a new society with a different culture, its members cling to their former way of life." I submit that this is an intelligible statement, if not a profound one, and that the essential meaning of the original (if I understand it) remains intact.[2]

Another negative illustration of the virtue of simplicity, briefer than the first but hardly less impressive, is to be found in an affidavit of Mr. Nixon's physician concerning the illness of the former President: "This post-operative complication was of such a magnitude as could have resulted in a terminal event." An English translation might read: "This complication could have been fatal."

This particular sentence is not only wordy and pompous, it is deliberately blurred. "A terminal event" is easier to face than "death," and in some cases it might be appropriate. It brings to the mind no unpleasant picture—in fact, no picture at all. Good writing, on the other hand, brings readers face to face with reality, whether pleasant or unpleasant. Its aim, as Joseph Conrad says in his Preface to *The Nigger of the Narcissus*, is "to make you hear, to make you feel—it is, before all, to make you *see*." It looks for words that are specific rather than general, concrete rather than abstract. It does not tell us that the girl *went* along the path but that she *tripped* or *skipped* or *danced*. It does not tell us that she was *pretty*, but that she had *dimples, clear blue eyes* with *friendly crinkles at the corners*, a mouth with *a humorous twist*.

Even when a writer is dealing with ideas rather than people, defending a thesis rather than telling a story, he needs to give his readers something for the imagination to take hold of and work on, some links with the world of the senses and the emotions. He will not leave "patriotism," for instance, as an abstraction without any content except the power to stir a vague emotion, but will help the reader to relate it to particular effects—perhaps a throb of the heart at the sight of the flag, a lump in the throat at the singing of the national anthem, a surge of devotion in the presence of the nation's leader. Or perhaps a tide of resentment against the failure to acknowledge the gulf between our vaunted ideals and the brutal reality—an eye only for the pollution of the "spacious skies," for strip-mining and clear-cutting on the slopes of "purple mountain majesties," for oil-slicks on the "shining sea," for crime and grime

---

[2] In TV interviews that I have witnessed since, Mr. Moynihan's language has often been simple and lucid.

in the "alabaster cities," for the sweat and dirt and aching muscles and squalid shelters and scanty wages of many of those who till the "fruited plain," for a "success" measured in terms of money and power however acquired instead of "nobleness," for racial hatred instead of "brotherhood." Or perhaps a level look at both the sordidness and splendor which surround us, and a resolute hope of diminishing the one and adding to the other.

This is to say that when a writer uses an abstract term, he recognizes—if he is a good writer—that his audience will not know what he means until it is told in terms of specific feelings and actions, until the abstraction is made concrete.

So with "ethnic collectivity." At a guess, it refers to an inherited culture peculiar to a certain group—perhaps including foods and drinks, songs and dances, holiday celebrations; ceremonies associated with birth and marriage and death; relations between husbands and wives, parents and children, adolescent boys and girls. But how are we to *know*, unless the writer lifts the curtain of abstraction and lets us *see* the living people that it hides?

And of course it is not only in writings about people that concrete examples are essential. Even such a seemingly mechanical and impersonal process as dictionary-making often involves the use of illustrative quotations to clarify the meaning of a word. An abstract definition of a word often leaves the reader puzzled; he needs to see it *used*. Composition textbooks, also, are filled with examples of what the student is being urged to do or to avoid doing.[3] Indeed, any good textbook, in whatever field, illustrates each principle as it is presented. In biology, for instance, an explanation of the Darwinian theory of evolution by natural selection would inevitably involve a discussion of its working in a particular species. (I remember from my introductory botany course the example of spots on the castor bean!)

Of course, abstractions are necessary. The very existence of reason depends on the ability to generalize, to categorize, to derive a uniform principle from a number of separate instances. Without this faculty we should be like Swift's inventors (in Book III of *Gulliver's Travels*) of a convenient substitute for speech, which involves so many difficulties and dangers. Each person prepares and

---

[3] The reader will note—I hope only now when it is called to his attention, since illustrations should be unobtrusive—that in this essay general statements are regularly accompanied by examples.

CLARITY

carries with him a pack of all the objects that he may wish to refer to in conversation, and when two persons meet, their method of communication is to put down their packs, pick out the objects that they have in mind, and display them to each other.

But though any serious writer must sometimes deal with abstract principles and general truths, he will carry with him a stock of concrete words and will have at his command a store of specific examples to link the world of thought and theory to the world of the senses and of actions. Seeing is believing, as television has recently reaffirmed. Books about the Vietnam war, however vividly written, awakened Americans only gradually to the ignorance, the folly, the lies of their leaders. But the visual impact could be less easily ignored.

Still, few of us have access to a TV audience; we have to do the best we can with language alone. And in doing so we have to recognize that Conrad's creed for the literary artist is equally valid for any user of words who wishes to influence other members of his society. He must make them *see*.

Besides depending on the choice of words—words that are exact, simple, and concrete—and the selection of telling illustrations—clarity demands no less painstaking care in showing how they are related to each other, which words go with which other words. This is mainly a matter of consistency, of holding to a certain point of view, of seeing each sentence as a whole and making sure that every essential part is present and in its proper place.

The failure of many students in composition classes to follow this procedure has added greatly to the list of things that teachers and textbooks have traditionally told them, sometimes justifiably, not to do. No object of absolutist attack, for instance, has been more mercilessly belabored than the "dangling participle"—the most ill-famed of a group of siblings known as "dangling modifiers." These are phrases—which usually contain a verb form but may be simple prepositional phrases—which the writer has inadvertently left hanging in the air with no visible means of support; that is, without any specific word to modify. The result is that the modifier attaches itself, following a normal principle of English, to the nearest word that is grammatically acceptable, usually a noun or pronoun. The effect is often ludicrous.

A classic example, which even students have sometimes chuckled over, is: "Riding down the hill on my bicycle, the town hall struck my eye." Taken literally, this sentence says that the town hall, having appropriated the writer's bicycle, came riding down the hill on it and hit him in the eye. If this were pointed out to him, he might try again, and produce the following: "Riding down the hill on my bicycle, my eye fell on the town hall." Eventually he could probably be brought to see the desirability of telling the reader who was doing the riding: "Riding down the hill on my bicycle, *I saw the town hall.*"

In the same class is this specimen from a medical column in the Chicago *Tribune* (a paper that heaped heavy editorial sarcasm on my original innocent advice to English teachers): "While acquiring the habit of standing or walking as tall as possible, the feet should be used properly." Equally at odds with the normal order of existence was the statement of one of my students in an essay entitled "Something About Myself": "At the age of eight, my mother married again."

That the result is so often ridiculous is perhaps the reason why dangling modifiers get so much attention. In practice, however, they are not a major source of difficulty. Even in extreme cases we can usually see what the author intended to say, and we habitually accept without question usages which a strict application of traditional rules would force us to say are wrong. A composition teacher would hardly be discharged for telling his students: "In writing a theme, the first requirement is having something to say." A golf instructor would not be pronounced incompetent for saying: "In putting, it is important to keep the head down." Massachusetts Income Tax Officials evidently thought the following instruction would be clear: "If using Form 1A and married, a joint return must be filed."

Even literary classics are full of dangling modifiers. One that has stuck in my mind is a famous passage by Alexander Pope, who gave his name to an "age" (the early eighteenth century) of English literature:

> Vice is a creature of such frightful mien
> As, to be hated, needs but to be seen.
> But seen too oft, familiar with her face,
> We first endure, then pity, then embrace.

I do not recall that "seen," though obviously mismated with "we," has been reprehended by any editor or critic.

CLARITY

Still, it bothers *me*—a little. Again, the question is not what is acceptable, but what is best. To separate the *doing* from the *doer*, or (as in the last example, where the modifier is a past participle) what is *done* from the thing that it is *done to*, can serve no purpose, and may demand of the reader a needless readjustment of his point of view. Why not exercise the minimum care required to be consistent? "In writing a theme, you must first have something to say." "In putting, keep your head down." "If using Form 1A and married, you must file a joint return." I will not venture to rewrite Pope, but *he* could have done better.

Less often provocative of mirth, but a more frequent obstacle to clarity, are pronouns that also "dangle," and make the reader guess what they refer to. If we read, "The country was divided by the Vietnam war, which was a great misfortune," we do not know which was the misfortune, the war itself or the division which it caused. Some persons might ask, since the general drift is clear, "Does it matter?" The answer is that it *does*—that it is always the writer's duty to say (within the limits imposed by the nature of the language itself) *exactly* what he means.

And if the sentence above is followed by, "This led to many protest meetings and marches," the mental smog grows thicker. *What* led to the protest—the division, the war, the misfortune, or some unmentioned general *malaise* that the reader is assumed to have in mind? The proper assumption, however, is that the reader does not know more than he has been told, and that it is unfair to make him track down, or guess at, references that ought to be unmistakable. I used to tell students never to use a pronoun that did not refer to one specific word. This was unreasonable (nobody can object to *this* "this"—though the sentence would not be harmed if "this" were followed by "order" or "command" or "prohibition" or "precept" or "rule"), but anyone who cares for excellence in writing will see the need to ask, concerning every use of "this" or "which" or "it," "Is the reference absolutely clear?" Here, as always, it is not enough to produce a passage that can be understood; the aim must be a passage that cannot be misunderstood.

Dangling modifiers and vague pronouns are two examples of the need to make clear the relations between words. There are many others, but these will make the point.

And from this point we may proceed to the next, namely, the need to make clear the relation between more inclusive units of content. This is what the textbooks call "coherence." I remember that in my high school composition text the author kept reiterating the importance—in sentences, paragraphs, and whole compositions—of "unity, coherence, and emphasis." I did not then understand the last two terms, but when—in trying to teach other people—I did learn their meaning, I recognized that he was right.

Unity hardly needs explaining. I understood it even as a high school student. Anybody who cannot see when materials are related and when they are not, and who, when the principle has been explained, cannot put related items together and keep unrelated items apart, really deserves Mr. Morse's judgment on someone who fails to make subjects and verbs agree. He "cannot think clearly." Anyone who would write something like "Ms. Smith was a beautiful young woman, and she always voted Republican" is probably beyond help. Many things might be mentioned about Ms. Smith that would have some relation to her beauty, but her voting habits are not among them. (I wonder what happened to my student who wrote, "I was born in 1938 and am very interested in sports.")

Coherence comes into the picture—or rather fails to come into the picture—when the thing that brings the reader up short is not a real lack of unity but only a lack of continuity, a failure by the writer to show the connection between successive statements. Since this connection is clear in his own mind, he too easily assumes that it will be apparent to the reader. The obvious analogy is once more with a road that is poorly marked, where one comes upon a curve without warning or is confronted with a fork or a crossroad without a sign.

The most common signposts in writing fall into certain groups. One tells the reader that the line of thought will continue in a certain direction, that the next sentence will amplify or clarify what has just been said. "And," "also," "moreover," "furthermore," "then," "next," "second," "in addition," "in fact," "indeed"—these are some of the ways of saying, "Keep straight ahead." "Another group prepares the reader for a change in the point of view or the direction of the thought. "But," "however," "nevertheless," "on the other hand," "to be sure"—these and others like them say, "Slow —curve." A third group indicates that the following sentence will state a result of some earlier condition or action: "therefore," "consequently," "accordingly," "hence," "thus," "so," "as a result," "it follows." Next, there are the commonplace phrases that introduce an illustration: "for example," "for instance," "let us say." Finally (not that the analysis is exhaustive), if the writer sees no need to indicate a particular relation but merely wishes to show *a* relation, he may rely on the pronouns "this" and "such."

These are some of the brief and obvious connectives available to a writer once he is aware of the problem. And if, among this wealth of possibilities, none seems exactly right, there are of course any number of more subtle and circuitous means of keeping the reader on the track.

There is more to coherence, however, than verbal links. It is not enough that each successive sentence should be in some way attached to the one preceding; there is always some natural principle of progression that the reader should be able to find and follow. It may be chronological—from an earlier "point in time" to a later, or a later to an earlier; or spatial—from what is low to what is high or what is near to what is distant, or the reverse of each; or logical—from the particular to the general or from the general to the particular; or rhetorical—from statement to restatement, or from abstract assertion to supporting illustration. Or some other organizing principle may be invoked, depending on the subject matter and the writer's purpose.

Let us suppose that a student in a political science course was asked in an examination to summarize the 1972 Presidential election. Suppose that he had a good memory and so had the main facts in mind, but that he had had little practice in writing essay examinations or in organizing his thoughts when working under pressure. The result might be something like this.

"In the 1972 Presidential election the Republican candidate, Richard Nixon, defeated the Democratic candidate, George McGovern. McGovern was a weak candidate, and the election was the most one-sided in American history. McGovern made a mistake in picking his Vice Presidential candidate, Senator Eagleton. He did not know that Eagleton had once suffered a nervous breakdown, and he could not decide what to do when this became known. The man he finally picked, Sargent Shriver, had never been in a political election. Besides, McGovern made many enemies in his own party during the primaries and at the National Convention. Nixon had no serious opposition in the primaries or at the Republican National Convention.

"McGovern tried to make the Vietnam war an issue. He had

done this in the primaries and it had worked. He also accused the Nixon administration of being the most corrupt in the nation's history. Most people did not take this charge seriously. Nixon did not campaign. Instead, he let his 'surrogates' make the speeches. They attacked McGovern as a radical. Nixon stood for law and order. People were worried about student riots and about drug use and violent crimes. They associated these with McGovern. Nixon was skillful in appealing to people who were against busing for school integration and against abortion. It also seemed as if at last he was ending the Vietnam war, as he had promised.

"Another thing that most people approved of was his visit to Communist China. He was also helped by the attempt to assassinate Wallace. People who would have voted for Wallace now had nobody to vote for except Nixon. McGovern had lost the support of George Meany, head of the AFL-CIO, because of his stand on the war and also his reputation as a radical. Meany ordered his unions not to support the Democratic candidate. People were sick of hearing about the war and of all the things that were wrong with the country. Nixon made them feel secure. He got more than 60 per cent of the popular vote and all the electoral votes except those from Massachusetts and the District of Columbia."

In this discussion the writer's thoughts are apparently put down at random,[4] with no attempt to organize or connect them, although they are all relevant to the general topic. If we take a little time to reflect, however, the materials almost arrange themselves. The natural starting point is the result, which naturally calls for an explanation: first, in terms of the events and forces working against McGovern, and then in terms of those working for Nixon. Finally, some kind of general summing up, some attempt to bring the whole picture into focus, is needed. On this plan, the material might be reworked as follows.[5] (I have added a few rhetorical refinements.)

---

[4] In fact, I had to make an effort to be non-consecutive, and may have overdone it. But I think the passage bears a reasonable resemblance to what might be produced by a well-informed but inexperienced student working under pressure. It seems to me that I have read thousands of similarly mixed-up answers to examination questions.

[5] Other arrangements are of course possible, as in almost any piece of expository writing. One would be to pick out the main topics—pre-convention events, the conduct of the conventions, the relations between the candidates

CLARITY

"In the 1972 election, the Republican candidate, Richard Nixon, defeated the Democratic candidate, George McGovern, in the most one-sided Presidential contest in the history of the United States. Nixon won more than 60 per cent of the popular vote and all the electoral votes except those of Massachusetts and the District of Columbia.

"To some McGovern supporters this result remains incredible, but it is not inexplicable. McGovern's victories in the primaries embittered some of his rivals and their supporters, and the party was further divided by events at the National Convention, where many 'regulars' were humiliated by McGovern's 'amateurs.' To these liabilities were added the candidate's personal indecisiveness, which was dramatically demonstrated by his handling of the Eagleton affair. When he learned that the man he had chosen for Vice President had a history of mental illness, he wavered painfully between support and dismissal, and then was slow and fumbling in the choice of a substitute, Sargent Shriver, who had never been a candidate in a political election. Perhaps a still greater handicap was the success of his opponents in representing him as a 'radical' (he was in fact a liberal in the traditional mold), the candidate of 'hippies,' 'draft-dodgers,' drug addicts, and other dissident groups. This caricature frightened many middle-class voters, and, along with his opposition to the Vietnam war, incurred the hostility of George Meany, who ordered the AFL-CIO unions not to support him. Moreover, the Vietnam issue, which had won him the nomination, failed him in the election, since Nixon seemed about to keep his promise to end American involvement.

"This apparent success made plausible Nixon's pose as a statesman rather than a politician, too busy with world affairs to spend time in defending himself or criticizing his opponent; these tasks were left to 'surrogates,' who would take responsibility for any tactical errors. Even more influential in creating the image of a world leader was his trip to China, which was applauded by everybody but a handful of right-wing fanatics. At the same time, he was, unlike McGovern, in complete control of his party. He had

---

and other leaders of their respective parties, the organization and management of the campaign, the ideological issues, the non-candidacy of Wallace—and discuss each in turn with reference to both candidates.

no serious opposition in any primary, and inside the Convention hall there was not a whisper of dissent. As for issues, he won additional support by his skillful exploitation of anti-crime, anti-busing-for-school-integration (both mainly euphemisms for "anti-black"), and anti-abortion sentiments that were increasingly rampant in much of the country. Ironically, the event that probably helped him most was purely fortuitous, namely, the attempted assassination of George Wallace, which left millions of right-wing voters with no choice except the Republican candidate.

"Beyond all these specific factors was the mood of the American people. Torn by fears and hatreds, weary of the war and its unconfessed burden of guilt, they wanted to forget the evils of the past, evade the problems of the present, be assured of security and prosperity in the future; to be comforted, praised, and relieved of responsibility by a strong and confident leader. The last thing they wanted to hear was a rehearsal of past errors, a summons to repent of present sins, a call for a strenuous crusade against social ills—and all this from a man who seemed uncertain, indecisive, unable to lead even his own party. The outcome was inevitable."

Whatever its merits or demerits as a political analysis, this passage is, I think, coherent. The material is now ordered, and the sentences are connected. The reader will have no difficulty in following the thought, and so can concentrate on deciding how far it is valid.

I hope, also, that the reader will find the language in general to be pointed, plain, and concrete, the broad assertions supported by specific examples, and modifiers and pronouns visibly linked to the persons or things that they refer to.

6
NATURALNESS

If the first virtue of style is clarity, the second is naturalness. Writing can be clear and yet dulled and deadened by restraint and circumspection. On the other hand, lack of clarity may be due to a lack of naturalness—to needlessly technical terminology or to literary pretentiousness. Or, instead of the writer's careless use of words incomprehensible to ordinary readers, or the deliberate desire to impress such readers by his skill in verbal jugglery and sleight of hand, the difficulty may lie in his inclination to refine and qualify and dissect until the thought vanishes in the maze presented to the baffled reader.

Of course, "natural"—along with its derivatives—is a tricky term. The natural speech and writing of persons who have done little reading or thinking is usually vague, awkward, trite, and generally ineffective, punctuated frequently by "you know," when in fact the audience does *not* know what the person is trying to say. The ultimate illustration of this kind of naturalness is the Watergate tapes. The language of Nixon and his fellow conspirators is unbelievably smudged, fumbling, disjointed, banal—inexpressive to the last degree. In a very different way, it is natural, perhaps, for specialists to speak and write what to the rest of us is unintelligible. The naturalness for which I am here contending (and which I shall try to define more fully later on) is the way sensitive and thoughtful people use language unselfconsciously in sharing information or ideas that will be of interest to like-minded persons.

It is naturalness in this sense that justifies many usages that absolutists condemn. It is natural, for instance, to say "the reason is because..." even though a strict application of traditional grammar would demand "the reason is that...." "Because," the absolutist argument runs, properly introduces an adverbial clause modifying a verb expressive of action: "He came because he was curious." On the other hand, "the reason is" ought to be followed by a noun construction—a clause beginning with "that." "The reason he came was that he was curious." But in people's actual speech we almost always hear, and in their writing often see, "The reason he came was because he was curious." It is natural to start an explanation with "The reason is"; and then it is also natural, after a half-pause while the explanation is being formulated in the reader's mind, to re-emphasize the causal relation. A person is asked: "What was your reason for refusing the offer?" And the answer follows an almost automatic formula: "The reason I refused was because I didn't like the terms."

Even more natural, perhaps, is the use of a "because"-clause at the beginning of a sentence, as its subject. A noted editor of Emily Dickinson, with impeccable scholarly credentials, comments: "Because she could be whimsical about the things that mattered most is no reason for ignoring the forces from which her strength was drawn." Because this natural, clear, and free-flowing sentence contains a technical violation of traditional grammar is no reason for condemning it.

Of course I am not suggesting that there is anything *un*natural about "the reason is that..."; I myself prefer it—because I was taught to, and it has long been a habit. It is natural to *me*. But I am sure that I am in the minority, even among (let us say) university faculty members.

Here I may as well complete my answer to those who accuse me, and other pragmatists, of failing to follow in our own writing the patterns that we justify in general. I confess that I often use "shall," and "whom," and "he" after the verb "to be," and the "contrary-to-fact subjunctive" ("if I were he"), and other forms dear to the absolutists. I use them because I learned to use them long ago, when I was young, and learned the lesson well, so that it is natural for me to use them now. To deliberately avoid them would be an affectation—though sometimes when I think about it I choose "who" instead of "whom" as a matter of principle; and I *always* think

NATURALNESS

about "different than," because the decree against it is so absurd. (I have used it so often that it now seems almost natural!)

An appeal to naturalness will also reverse the verdict passed by absolutists on "like" as a conjunction, in place of "as." Of course one can sympathize with their irritation at the notorious "Winston tastes good, like a cigarette should"; the unmitigated hokum employed by the tobacco industry to sell a product and encourage a habit that is enslaving, unclean, costly, dangerous, and offensive to many of those who have not succumbed to it, is surely one of the shabbiest violations of taste and morality to be found even in a system where profits are more important than people. But this does not sustain the dogma that such a use of "like" is ungrammatical.[1] Language that everybody—or almost everybody—uses *must* be grammatically correct, since (to risk again the charge of tiresome repetition) grammar is only a systematic description of the way language is used.

In this instance, moreover, the common usage seems perfectly reasonable. In showing a person how to do something, we pass naturally from "Do it like this" to "Do it like I do." When a boy expresses admiration of his idol in basketball or hockey, does "I wish I could shoot like him" sound more natural—or better in any other way—than "I wish I could shoot like he does"? When we say, "She sings like an angel," are we not really saying, "She sings like an angel sings"? Is this any different than what we do in trying to explain that in the sentence "She sings better than he" (instead of "him") the verb "sings" is "understood" at the end, and the full statement is "She sings better than he sings"? Or if we say that a garment "looks like new," would not the full sentence be (if we insist on explaining the grammar) "It looks like it is new"? On what authority is it asserted that when we supply the verb that was previously "understood," we must change "like" to "as" or "as if"?

Especially in the latter case, where the absolutist preference

---

[1] One shudders to contemplate the effect on objectors to the Winston line of a less familiar (perhaps derivative) slogan advertising a different brand (More): "It fits your face like it found a home." As for my own reaction to this alliterative impudence, I find it impossible to suppress a grin. Incidentally, the reader may notice the use of the simple past tense "found" where "had found" would be traditional. A parallel instance is "caught" in the sentence quoted below.

would be for "as if," many people find it natural to use "like." "He looks like he had been in a fight" or "He acts like he owned the place" or "It looks like we're going to have a storm" are certainly good informal English. So is the following sentence from a *New York Times Magazine* article on orthodontics, in which the author comments on an appliance called a "tooth positioner": "the child wearing one looks like he caught a hockey puck in the teeth." Using "as if" for "like" would take half the fun out of the sentence. Similarly, though in a somewhat more serious vein, the Boston *Globe* quotes a teacher who had asked the members of her kindergarten class to draw pictures of their families: "The families didn't look like ours did."

If it is objected that these instances are representative of informal use, it is easy enough to find examples in serious, formal writing. In an article in the *New York Times Book Review,* a professor of government at Harvard observes (I think justly) that "Arabs behave like the rest of us would under similar circumstances." And a well known writer on nature comments in an *Audubon* magazine article: "Our minds and senses absorbed [a bird's song] half-consciously, unquestioningly, like those who love and understand good music absorb and take for granted the intricate composition of a favorite symphony." Or we can turn to a classic of English fiction, D. H. Lawrence's *Sons and Lovers,* for the following simile: "like the Trent carries bodily its backswirlings and intertwinings, noiselessly."

And so what if 75 per cent of the *American Heritage* "panel of experts" find this usage "unacceptable"? Unacceptable to who? (I like "who" in this context.) Do the experts *own* the English language? Have they ever read, one wonders wickedly, Noah Webster's remark about "our hypercritics, who are very apt to distrust popular practice, and substitute their own rules for customs founded on common sense"?

There are many other expressions used naturally by many literate persons though proscribed by absolutist "experts," but I resist the temptation to mention more than a few. One which must not be passed over is "cannot help but." It is depressing to reflect how much red ink and energy have been wasted in trying to make students avoid this natural, clear, and vigorous phrase. (I wasted some myself when I was young and when, to a certain extent, I shared with my students the innocent belief that a textbook writer always

NATURALNESS

knows what he is talking about.) "I cannot help but think that Spiro Agnew should have gone to jail" is acceptable to most intelligent people in form as well as substance. Traditional textbooks prescribe "cannot but think" or "cannot help thinking"; the former however, verges on affectation, and although I myself (to the best of my knowledge) habitually use the latter, most people seem to feel unconsciously that "but" lends added emphasis. At any rate, they obviously feel at ease in using it.

Another traditional object of absolutist antipathy has been a preposition at the end of a sentence. Though I doubt that many persons still take it seriously (even Sheridan Baker and Wilson Follett, as far as I can discover, do not mention it), perhaps there are still those who need to be gently told that no self-respecting writer or speaker has ever bothered to conform to this most errant of all imagined rules of "grammar."

To prick this bubble of misbelief, we can (for the benefit, especially, of those persons who are tender toward the past), quote Shakespeare at almost any length. To take *Hamlet* alone, the Ghost "would be spoke to" (Bernardo, not being a "scholar" like Horatio, can be forgiven for not saying "spoken"); what Hamlet's trouble may be, the King "cannot dream of"; Polonius, on the same topic, opines that Hamlet's love of Ophelia is the cause of his madness and "all we wail for"; Rosencrantz and Guildenstern confess, finally, that they "were sent for"; and in the most famous soliloquy in English drama, Hamlet himself makes somber mention of the painful "shocks / That flesh is heir to," but notes that most people "would rather bear those ills we have / Than fly to others that we know not of."

If a modern instance is desired, there is the famous story of Winston Churchill's annihilation of some mistaught underling who rashly "corrected" a Churchillian sentence that ended with a preposition: "This is the kind of arrant nonsense up with which I will not put."

Another innocent victim of the prejudice that a preposition should always precede its object was a student in one of my classes in Freshman English who, describing his loneliness in college, especially for his girl-friend, wrote: "I never stop worrying as to with whom she's kicking up her heels now." The metaphor, though familiar, is in this context delightful. But how much better if, uninhibited by (I suppose) the remembered admonitions of his high school English teacher, he had written: "I never stop worrying about who she's kicking up her heels with now."

A final instance of a natural expression now widely used which arouses the wrath of absolutists is "hopefully" as a substitute for "it is to be hoped." In discussing Middle Eastern politics, one might say: "Hopefully, Arabs and Israelis will eventually come to tolerate each other." This seems to me natural, clear, convenient, and economical; and these virtues are not outweighed by the traditional use of the word to describe a particular act by a particular person, as in "He waited hopefully." Though some of my best friends rage against the innovation, I judge that their anger results from an unreflective antipathy to what is new and popular, no matter how useful.

Some readers not persuaded of the merits of naturalness by these examples of varied usages will perhaps be more kindly disposd toward some negative instances of the same general principle. As a department head I once received the following letter from a candidate for a position.

> I received a communication from _____ College today, importing that I had been proposed for an instructorship in English at _____ University. Permit me to assure you that I regard this position with profound interest, both as a path toward what I have long esteemed the most precious amenities of human life, and as a means to the fulfilment of a dream conceived scarcely beyond the verge of boyhood.
>
> It is with a tolerably clear view of what college teaching requires that I venture upon this application. I should not have presumed to aspire so high, were I not sustained by the asseverations of my preceptors at _____, that I do actually possess some of the imponderables of personality which inform the college instructor.
>
> All necessary documents concerning me will be transmitted to you at once by _____ College. I shall await your decision with sincere interest; and meanwhile, in the hope that this overture may eventuate in a mutually promising association, remain
>
> Very truly yours,[2]

[2] Legally, a letter belongs to the writer, and may not be published without his permission. But should the writer of this letter happen to see it, I hope

NATURALNESS

It can be said at least for this letter that the reader does not have to struggle to grasp its meaning. This is more than can be said for some famous critics of literature (whose profession, one might suppose, would have given them some feeling for English style). R. P. Blackmur, for instance, burdens his readers with the task of interpreting passages like these. "What obstructs us [in Thomas Hardy's poetry] . . . is a thicket of ideas, formulas, obsessions, indisciplined compulsions, nonce insights, and specious particularities." "He failed to recognize and failed to absorb those modes of representing felt reality persuasively and credibly and justly, which make up, far more than meters and rhymes and the general stock of versification, the creative habit of imagination, and which are the indefeasible substance of tradition." [3] An earnest effort to penetrate *this* thicket of interwoven abstractions and entangling strange alliances of ponderous and uncommon words ("thicket" is the only concrete and readily graspable term in either sentence) leaves me still on the outside looking in, trying to reach the thought whose outlines are only dimly and tantalizingly visible.

These passages, of course, suffer from a different kind of unnaturalness than appears in the letter. The cause is not naiveté, but an excess of sophistication. The author is not thinking about impressing the reader; his aim is clearly to share his perceptions and opinions. One might even say that he tries too hard. Fearful of over-simplifying or of not being exhaustive, he keeps adding one noun to another, one verb to another, an adjective to a noun, three adverbs with slightly different meanings for the reader to juggle in his mind, a qualifying phrase within a qualifying clause. One gropes for a simple statement to lay hold of, a friendly everyday word among the unsmiling formal crowd. It is natural, too, to expect an occasional illustration to help one come to grips with whatever it is that lies behind such epithets as "nonce insights" and "specious particularities."

---

he will forgive me for putting it to a use that I am sure he will now, after some thirty years, approve. Despite the vocabulary, I got the impression that he was a likable person; and though we never got better acquainted, since there were more promising candidates, I wrote to one of the persons who had recommended him (a noted scholar and teacher) to suggest that he give the applicant some fatherly advice about writing letters of application. I received a pleasant and appreciative answer, and hope there was a happy outcome.

[3] *Form and Value*, pp. 2, 9. Later in the book we are confronted by such intimidating verbal monsters as "enantiodromia" and "plurisignativeness."

One might perhaps try to defend Mr. Blackmur by saying that his style is "natural" to *him*. This takes us back to the beginning, and the need for a generally applicable concept of naturalness in communication. A tentative definition of such a concept might include the following items. First, it involves an honest desire to communicate, a constant conviction of the worth of what one has to say. It does not seek to inflate a trivial subject matter, nor devalue a significant one, in order to make an occasion for rhetorical display. Second, it involves a respect for words as well as for the subject matter, a refusal to degrade them through mindless repetition into faceless counters, empty sounds, meaningless marks. Such shoddy use of language is "natural" only to the unthinking. Third, it involves respect for the audience, and not only respect but considerateness. It does not, like Mr. Blackmur in the quoted passages, indulge a private punctiliousness in the choice of words, which unduly burdens, if it does not completely baffle, even the serious reader.

The staggering failure to meet these moderate demands, or even to be conscious of them, on the part of those who ought to be our leaders—persons in public life, powerful figures in business and industry, representatives of the media, even on occasion academics and other intellectuals—has been documented in appalling though sometimes hilarious abundance by Edwin Newman in *Strictly Speaking*. Redundancy and repetition, reliance on clichés, conscious or unconscious evasion of issues through use of meaningless jargon —these are an affront alike to any serious subject matter, to the language, and to the audience; they are tolerable only because we have been battered by them for so long that we are only half aware of what is going on.

Here I will only add a sort of exclamation point to Mr. Newman's account. We have all watched and listened to televised press conferences or interviews participated in by eminent persons from a President down (or possibly sometimes *up*), and perhaps have at some time heard one of them say, in answer to the rare question that is simple and direct, "Yes" or "No." If my own experience is typical, we have responded with the kind of involuntary laughter that is triggered by something totally unexpected, some dramatic departure from the normal pattern; and then with an impulse to applaud an action that ought to be so natural and is in fact almost eccentric.

NATURALNESS

It is not surprising, therefore, that "eccentric" is an epithet often applied to the writer to whom I turn for an instance of a natural style. This is Thoreau; and if he pressed too hard his contention that to be truly natural is the surest way to earn this epithet, it is indisputable that his writing measures up to the standard of naturalness that I have set. If some critics have alleged that his conduct was tainted by affectation, they cannot say so of his style.

I left the woods [he writes toward the end of *Walden*] for as good a reason as I went there. Perhaps it seemed to me that I had several more lives to live, and could not spare any more time for that one. It is remarkable how easily and insensibly we fall into a particular route, and make a beaten track for ourselves. I had not lived there a week before my feet wore a path from my door to the pond-side; and though it is five or six years since I trod it, it is still quite distinct. It is true, I fear, that others may have fallen into it, and so helped to keep it open. The surface of the earth is soft and impressible by the feet of men; and so with the paths which the mind travels. How worn and dusty, then, must be the highways of the world, how deep the ruts of tradition and conformity!

In some sense, as Thoreau suggests, it is "natural" for people to stay in the ruts. But in my sense, as well as his, naturalness demands that we stay out; but not that we look down on or lose touch with our fellow travelers on the uneven highway of human life.

7
FORCEFULNESS

It is evident that naturalness goes hand in hand with clarity. But with a third stylistic virtue, forcefulness,[1] it may be either allied or in conflict. This is what, in my high school textbook, was called "emphasis," and I suppose I failed to understand it because it is, after all, a bit difficult to explain or define. It is not necessarily achieved in speech by shouting or a clenched fist, nor in writing by using weighty words or startling figures of speech; but by putting together sentences, or larger units, in which sound and stress and movement and meaning reinforce each other.

Forcefulness comes first of all from economy. Nothing destroys it more surely than superfluous words. Even the handbooks all agree that wordiness is a fatal vice. It is true that some redundant expressions have become so habitual that we accept them with no sense of unpleasant iteration, as when we unconsciously attach "up" or "down" to a familiar verb. Perhaps another phrase approaching this condition, though still coldly viewed in many class-

---

[1] "Force" would be more forceful than "forcefulness" with its extra unstressed syllables. But "force" has overtones of violence, compulsion, aggression; it is something that we shrink from or angrily resist, that we resort to with reluctance. Busing of students to achieve racial integration in schools is always "forced busing" to its opponents, though it is their own racial bias that has created the need for compulsion; and the adjective automatically intensifies their opposition. In this discussion, as often, the choice of a word depends on balancing positive and negative values.

rooms, is "throughout the whole . . ." before a noun indicative of time, space, or process. Most readers and writers evidently feel that "whole" gives added emphasis. But in most similar expressions the result is just the reverse. To "continue on" instead of "continue," to "proceed to do" something instead of "do" it; to describe a person as "tall in stature" (as if one could be tall in girth or weight) or "honest in character" or "kind in nature" (as if the simple adjective were not enough); to say "at this point in time" for "at this point," or "at the present time" for "at present" (or perhaps either for simply "now"), or "during the time that" for "while," or "due to the fact that" for "because"—all these and many other ways of wasting words, though forgivable in casual conversation, usually add nothing but monotony to a writer's style.

Perhaps even more productive of dullness is the habit of repeating a sentence in different words while adding nothing to the substance. "As I have just said" may provoke the alert reader or hearer to the mental retort, "Then why say it again?" "In other words" is likely to prompt the question, "Why not have used the right words the first time?" To be sure, a subtle or complicated thought may need to be clarified by careful restatement. But too often, repetition is merely a habit—almost a reflex—inviting inattention or boredom from the reader or hearer.

There are other occasions where speakers (especially—but sometimes writers) do not even have the excuse of habit. They are simply not using their minds but only their vocal organs or their fingers. Of such behavior, Mr. Newman has also collected more than a few devastating examples. One that might be added to a later edition is the following oracular utterance of Britain's former Tory leader, Edward Heath (assuming that he was correctly quoted): "We must find a better way of finding a way out of our disputes."

Wordiness becomes especially oppressive when the unneeded words are ponderous, abstract, and technical or pseudo-technical. Whereas a stripped-down style carries the reader forward with no conscious exertion, such passages as the following require an almost physical effort to surmount the barriers to communication that the writer has heedlessly erected: "For all potential industrial conversion operations, the common requirement is the performance of a full redesign of the military-serving enterprise with the expectation that this must include major retraining and reorganization of occupations, as well as specific changes in the decision-making criteria that pervade the enterprise." [2]

This is jargon. Though the writer evidently knows what he wants to say (I even think *I* know what he wants to say), his preoccupation with the substance leads him to ignore the style. Like some enthusiastic but non-literary college freshman, he puts down the first words that occur to him—and leaves them. He does not stop to ask himself how his words will strike his readers (in this instance, like a mud-slide).

Making sense of the passage is not as hard as it looks. Mostly it is a matter of simply omitting superfluous words. Beyond this, only a few changes are needed to make it intelligible. A possible revision is: "Industrial conversion will require a full redesign of the military-serving enterprise, including training of workers for new jobs, as well as establishing new criteria for making decisions." [3]

The original passage is also a powerful negative illustration of the value, for forcefulness as for clarity, of short and simple words. One may recall, to be sure, the weighty eloquence of Milton's prose or the resounding words that Johnson was so fond of. Yet beside the stately march of *Areopagitica* ("I cannot praise a fugitive and cloistered virtue, unexercised and unbreathed . . .") we may put the impassioned statement at the end of *A Ready and Easy Way to Establish a Free Commonwealth*, published by Milton in defiance of the assured return of the Stuart monarchy and the likelihood of his execution for having urged and defended that of Charles I:

---

[2] Quoted in the *New York Times Book Review* from Seymour Melman, *The Permanent War Economy*. Mr. Melman's argument, as I gather from this and other reviews, is that the arms industry, often defended as a source of jobs and other economic benefits, is in fact destructive of the nation's economic health. It is a pity that such a thesis, which supports the misgivings of many ordinary citizens, is presented in a style that, if the quotation is typical, is virtually unreadable.

[3] The context would doubtless make clear that the conversion is from military to non-military production; if not, this phrase or a similar one would have to be added. "Military-serving enterprise" is a lead-shod phrase, but perhaps "weapons industry" would be too narrow. Or possibly one might borrow the phrase used by Eisenhower in a famous but unheeded warning: "the industrial-military complex" (putting it in quotation marks of course). Incidentally, the opening sentence of this paragraph as I first wrote it was: "The task of reducing the passage to readability is not as difficult as it looks." Rereading often helps.

FORCEFULNESS

"Thus much I should perhaps have said, though I were sure I should have spoken only to trees and stones, and had none to cry to, but with the prophet, 'O earth, earth, earth!' to tell the very soil itself what her perverse inhabitants are deaf to." And Johnson in his second most famous letter, responding to the bluster of James MacPherson, does not find a simple style "too easy": "I received your foolish and impudent letter. Any violence offered me I shall do my best to repel; and what I cannot do for myself, the law shall do for me. I hope I shall never be deterred from detecting what I think a cheat, by the menaces of a ruffian."

These passages recall a little essay published long ago in the *News-Letter* of the College English Association by a person whose name escapes my failing memory. The title, however, I remember: "Short Words Are Words of Might"; and the author forcefully defended his thesis in words of a single syllable.

I remember, too, the words of a neighbor in the rural community to which I still think of myself as in some measure belonging, as he considered the consequences of long life: "It's hard to be old." He was not what the dwellers in my other world would call an "educated" person; yet these five syllables distill the essence of all that has ever been said about the darker aspects of old age.

If forcefulness begins with choice of words, it is never fully achieved without attention to structure—to the way in which sentences, especially, but also paragraphs, are put together. The governing principle is that the strongest stress should fall automatically on the words or other elements that contribute most to the fulfillment of the author's aim.

This principle, in turn, depends upon two others. One is that the importance of an idea should determine the choice of the structural unit by which it is to be expressed—whether this unit should be a single word, a prepositional phrase, a verbal phrase, a subordinate clause, or a main clause. This process is sometimes spoken of as "subordination," and it can be studied in the following sentence: "As she stood in the doorway, facing the morning sun, her beauty was dazzling."

The principle demands that the main idea should be in the main clause, and it *is:* "Her beauty was dazzling." The next most important idea, "she stood in the doorway," is put in a subordinate clause. That she was "facing the morning sun" is assumed to have less claim to the reader's attention than that "she stood in the doorway."

(If the reverse were intended, the reading would be: "As she faced the morning sun, standing in the doorway. . . .") Next, where she happened to be standing—"in the doorway"—is seen as less important than how she was facing, and is given only a prepositional phrase. Finally, that she faced a "morning" (rather than a "noon," "afternoon," or "evening") sun is considered to be of still less moment. "Dazzling," to be sure, which is likewise only a single adjective, contains the heart of the sentence; but a word gains its significance from the context, and here "dazzling" modifies the subject of the main clause, "beauty." This is what the sentence is *about*—not the morning sun but a woman's dazzling beauty.

The second principle is that the stress that falls on a word or idea, and hence the force with which it is impressed on the mind of the audience, depends on its position in the sentence or paragraph. The strongest stress falls naturally at the beginning and at the end, and it is at these points that the important words or ideas are properly placed. Of the two positions, the last is most emphatic. (If I had said, "The last is the most emphatic of the two positions," the sentence would have been less forceful, since it would have ended with an unimportant word.)

These principles may be further clarified by the following sentences, which are identical except in arrangement. "He moved slowly and wearily as he went up the hill carrying his heavy burden." "As he went up the hill, carrying his heavy burden, he moved slowly and wearily." It is easy to see the difference in emphasis between these two sentences. In the first, the main thought (in the main clause) comes at the beginning and impresses itself on the reader's mind; but then the sentence trails off in details of less importance, expressed in structures of decreasing weight (a subordinate clause and a participial phrase). Here structure has more influence than position. Though "heavy burden" draws the reader's attention because it comes at the end, the fact that it has been relegated to a participial phrase diminishes the force of the impression. In the second sentence, on the other hand, both the structure and position of the items are appropriate to their apparent importance. The resulting statement is far more forceful.

A typical instance of an anticlimactic sentence ending, encountered with numbing frequency by every teacher of composition, is a verbal phrase beginning with "thus" and attached to the end of a sentence. The position suggests correctly that the content of the

FORCEFULNESS

phrase is the most important part of what the sentence has to say; but relegating it to a participial phrase—which, moreover, is often left "dangling" without a specific word to modify—destroys the forcefulness of the statement. Again, contrasting arrangements of sentence elements identical in content will make the point. One might say, in explaining the greatest air disaster that has yet occurred: "The plane crash was caused by a known but uncorrected structural defect, thus demonstrating the laxity of the Federal Aviation Administration." Or one might take thought and say: "The plane crash, caused by a known but uncorrected structural defect, demonstrates the laxity of the Federal Aviation Administration." The main thought is now in the main clause, and, moreover, does not have the appearance of an afterthought.

It should not be concluded that a "periodic" sentence (as the second pattern in each of the pairs of sentences is technically known) is always better than a "loose" sentence (one which follows the first pattern). Whereas a periodic sentence is usually more forceful, a loose sentence is often more natural. The danger in the latter, if the pattern is too often repeated, is that the reader may lose interest. The danger in the former, which, again, is heightened if the structure of successive sentences remains the same, is that the effect may seem contrived. There can be no absolute judgment as to which pattern is better. The "right" choice depends on the subject matter, the emotional tone, the position in a larger unit, and the total effect at which the writer is aiming.

It is the same relation between emphasis and position that underlies the objections sometimes raised to a preposition at the end of a sentence element and to a "split infinitive." As for the former, which has already been alluded to, the choice is, again, between a natural order which to some readers may seem unemphatic and a possibly more forceful order which will often seem artificial. Nobody would ask, "To what is the world coming?" rather than "What is the world coming to?"

The problem is the same in using an infinitive phrase. More stress usually falls on the modifier if it comes before "to" or after the verb, and if this is what the writer wants, that is where the modifier must go. But naturalness also has its claims, and it is sometimes more comfortable to insert the modifier between the "sign of the infinitive" and the verb proper. I would prefer to say, "To fully understand Watergate, one must understand Nixon's character" rather than "Fully to understand Watergate..." or "To understand Watergate fully...." It is no less clear, it is far more natural, and it is not (to my ear, at least) at all less forceful than the other versions. If it sounds "wrong," that is only because we have been, for no good reason, conditioned to avoid it.[4]

Besides the thoughtful ordering of sentence elements, there is another structural device whose contribution to forceful expression can hardly be overstated. This is "parallelism"—the presentation of successive items of subject matter in identical structures. It may be in the form of separate short sentences having the same pattern, or in the form of two or more words, phrases, or clauses within a single sentence, all related in the same way to the rest of the sentence. These sentence elements may be parallel in content as well as form, so that the effect is cumulative; or one element may be balanced by another of opposing import, so that the reader is struck by the contrast. In either case, the device can be extraordinarily effective when skillfully used. But it may also tempt a writer to over-indulgence, and then it is subject to the risks of both loose and periodic sentences. On the one hand, it may become monotonous; on the other, it may seem unnatural.

The classic example of a style made almost unreadable by artifice, especially an addiction to parallelism, is the *Euphues* of John Lyly, an early Elizabethan man of letters. Like many other Elizabethans, he was intoxicated with the English language, and in *Euphues* he sought to exhaust its possibilities in a certain direction. His great popular success added the word "euphuism" to the language. Here is a sample of what the word denotes.

> Though the beginning of love bring delight, the end bringeth destruction. For, as the first draft of wine doth comfort the stomach, the second inflame the liver, the third fume into the head, so the first sip of love is pleasant, the second perilous, the third pestilent. If thou perceive thyself to be enticed with their wanton glances, or allured with their wicked wiles, either en-

[4] Baker in *The Practical Stylist* quotes from George O. Curme's *English Grammar* examples of split infinitives from Ruskin, Arnold, Pater, Browning, and Oliver Wendell Holmes, and answers Curme's contention that "usage makes them right" by saying, "But each of them can be improved"—and then shows *how*, to his own satisfaction. Obviously Mr. Baker thinks he knows how God speaks English—or at least how He wants it to be spoken.

FORCEFULNESS

chanted with their beauty or enamoured of their bravery,[5] enter with thyself into this meditation: "What shall I gain if I obtain my purpose? Nay, rather, what shall I lose in winning my pleasure?"

A modern reader can take a little of this, as a curiosity; he may even, at first, admire the writer's ingenuity. But he soon sees that the style is only a facade, and that behind it there is neither original thought nor genuine feeling. That Lyly and his readers would probably have found this criticism beside the point only shows the narrowness of their view, their failure to perceive that (once more) language exists for communication, and that in serious writing, style is only a means to an end. As an end in itself, it is only a toy.[6]

On the other hand, excessive simplicity, also, sometimes results in a sort of parallelism that may strike the reader as being, like that in *Euphues*, both contrived and dull. This is a danger that Hemingway often flirts with, like a matador in his favorite sport—not always without injury. *In Our Time*, for instance, is full of one-line or half-line sentences of mostly one-syllable words. And sometimes, especially if he is willing occasionally to insert a longer sentence, the writing moves with ease and power. But sometimes it does not.

> It was a quiet night. The swamp was perfectly quiet. Nick stretched under the blanket comfortably. A mosquito hummed close to his ear. Nick sat up and lit a match. The mosquito was on the canvas, over his head. Nick moved the match quickly up to it. The mosquito made a satisfactory hiss in the flame. The match went out. Nick lay down again under the blanket. He turned on his side and shut his eyes. He was sleepy. He felt sleep coming. He curled up under the blanket and went to sleep.

If a college freshman were to submit a paper in this style, we would wonder why he was still writing at third-grade level. Hemingway, however, must be credited with knowing what he is doing. One supposes that he is trying to represent his character's consious-

---

[5] "Bravery" in Elizabethan English is a somewhat elusive word which has no exact modern equivalent. Here it means something like "boldness in displaying their charms."

[6] This position will be qualified in the following chapter.

ness as reduced to merely (as it would be, perhaps, in the given situation) a series of separate simple sensations and simple acts, undisturbed by anything resembling thought. He is also doubtless rebelling, consciously, against conventional literary taste.

Judgments as to the merit of the passage are bound to vary. My own response is exasperation at the minuteness and sameness of the units. It is as if one were forced to eat very small peas one at a time, or to walk along a railroad track stepping on each tie. It is unnatural, and it is monotonous. In the quoted passage, I would be happy if everything between the first sentence and the last were omitted.

Though our time is half a century later than Hemingway's, most serious writers seem to be still self-conscious, still suspicious of traditional eloquence, afraid to adopt familiar forms of so obvious a rhetorical device as parallelism, used so freely and confidently by the great writers of English prose in other centuries, to whom we may turn for examples.

A contemporary of John Lyly was Francis Bacon, whose style is almost as mannered as Lyly's in *Euphues*. It differs, however, in two respects. Bacon rigorously pruned the rhetorical luxuriance that Lyly cultivated for its own sake, and he did so because, unlike Lyly, he had something to say. Substance was more important than style. Yet the strictness of his economy, the precision with which he packed each sentence with thought, the firmness with which he ordered the march of his ideas, resulted inevitably in a style that was visibly artful as well as forceful. And both impressions—of artifice and forcefulness—are due largely to the use of parallelism.

Every student who has had to take a "survey course" in English literature has probably encountered Bacon's essay "Of Studies."

> Studies serve for delight, for ornament, and for ability. Their chief use for delight is in privateness and retiring; for ornament, is in discourse; and for ability, is in the judgment and disposition of business. For expert men can execute, and perhaps judge of particulars one by one; but the general counsels, and the plots and marshalling of affairs, come best from those that are learned. To spend too much time in studies is sloth; to use them too much for ornament is affectation; to make judgment wholly by their rules is the humour of a scholar. . . . Read not to contradict and confute; nor to believe and take for

FORCEFULNESS

granted; nor to find talk and discourse; but to weigh and consider. Some books are to be tasted, others to be swallowed, and some few to be chewed and digested.

No one can deny the vigor of this writing, nor the keenness of intellect which originates the thought and dictates the form. But students, I have found, do not usually warm up to Bacon, and one can see why. There is something mechanical, something bloodless, about the style. Naturalness is sacrificed to forcefulness.

Another English writer noted for the forcefulness of his style and for his use of parallelism and balance was the eminent Victorian Thomas B. Macaulay. As it happens, one of Macaulay's famous essays has for its subject Francis Bacon. Macaulay saw in Bacon greatness of intellect married to meanness of character; wisdom concerning humanity in general marred in practice by the "wisdom for a man's self" that in another essay Bacon analyzes as coldly and mercilessly as if he were not aware that (or so Macaulay contends in the quotation that follows) he is passing sentence upon himself.

> The difference between the soaring angel and the creeping snake was but a type of the difference between Bacon the philosopher and Bacon the Attorney-General, Bacon seeking for the truth and Bacon seeking for the Seals [belonging to the office of Lord Chancellor]. Those who survey only one half of his character may speak of him with unmixed admiration or with unmixed contempt. But those only judge of him correctly who take in at one view Bacon in speculation and Bacon in action.

Some readers may feel that this style is as artificial as Bacon's own—or even that of *Euphues*. But again there is a difference. In reading Macaulay one has no sense of self-conscious striving for effect. The resonant and rhythmic sentences seem to pour out of the author's mind and onto the page as effortlessly and naturally as a stream flows. One wonders, in fact, whether he should not sometimes have resisted the habit of casting his thoughts into such brilliantly balanced contrasts; whether his gift for seeing striking parallels, his eagerness to exploit dramatic possibilities, did not sometimes lead him to sacrifice substance to form, and distort a prosaic fact for the sake of an impressive phrase. Were Bacon's speculations always as lofty and his actions always as low as Macaulay would have us believe?

Here I myself must resist temptation—the temptation to keep on quoting famous passages of English prose. But since the style of each quotation so far given is somehow flawed, perhaps I may be allowed to present one passage that seems to me secure from adverse criticism. It is the beginning of John Henry Newman's sermon "The Second Spring."

> We have familiar experience of the order, the constancy, the perpetual renovation of the material world which surrounds us. Frail and transitory as is every part of it, restless and migratory as are its elements, never ceasing as are its changes, still it abides. It is bound together by a law of permanence, it is set up in unity, and though it is ever dying, it is ever coming to life again. Dissolution does but give birth to fresh modes of Organization, and one death is the parent of a thousand lives. Each hour, as it comes, is but a testimony, how fleeting, yet how secure, how certain, is the great whole. It is like an image on the waters, which is ever the same, though the waters ever flow.

It is unfair to quote so little. The sentences move across the page as evenly and powerfully as waves approaching the shore, each rising steadily to a climax and then yielding to its successor. And—what crowns the passage with perfection—the forcefulness of the style is sustained and certified by the faith of the mind that creates it. It is true that neither the faith nor the style, so disciplined and yet so free, is much in fashion in our chaotic age (not much more chaotic, however, than Newman's). But I insist that nostalgia has no part in my admiration of the passage.

A final element in the forceful use of language is imagery—that is, the attempt, by presenting one thing (object, action, sensation, emotion, concept) in terms of something else, to increase the measure and refine the quality of communication; to make the picture clearer, the impact more forceful. Perhaps such a comparison is with something more familiar than the original, to aid the reader's understanding; or with something strange and rare, to startle him to attention; or with something easier to visualize, or more accessible to the other senses, to involve him more fully in the experience that the writer wishes to share.

FORCEFULNESS

Though figures of speech are often thought of as belonging to poetry, they are used naturally in prose, and even in everyday speech. In fact, they are the source of many clichés because they have become habitual and automatic. To move "off like a shot," to "sleep like a log," to "drink like a fish"; or "lily-white" (not now used to describe a lady's hand but, in what might be called a second-degree metaphor, to indicate—often with a measure of contempt for a supposed excess of affectation—a person who is *morally* unsullied), "dog-eared," "beat-up," "dead-tired"—all these are figures of speech used constantly by persons who, if they ever heard of "simile" or "metaphor," have long since forgotten the definitions.[7]

Of course even sophisticated writers (such as former teachers of composition) often use imagery unconsciously. My comparison of Newman's sentences to waves was not a conscious prelude to a discussion of imagery; I was simply looking for some way to share with the reader my response to the passage, and so perhaps to make his perceptions richer and more rewarding. (Not that the latter thought, either, was in my mind. I was not trying to be edifying, but only helpful.)

Newman himself, in the passage quoted, is sparing of figures, but the two he uses—death as the parent of life and the physical world as an "image on the waters"—are fitting and memorable; not less so because the latter had been used before by Wordsworth and Shelley. The more melodramatic taste of Macaulay is manifest in his portrayal of the two sides of Bacon's character as "the soaring angel and the creeping snake"—a figure that also sticks in one's memory. Hardly less striking is Bacon's own use of imagery, as when, in a typically intellectual metaphor, he compares physical and mental food: "Some books are to be tasted, others to be swallowed, and some few to be chewed and digested."

Here, however, I raise a question. Is the figure, ingenious as it is,

---

[7] Imagery is mainly of two kinds: comparisons that are made explicit by the use of "like" or "as," and that are illustrated by the first group of illustrations above; and comparisons that are only implied, as in the second group. The first are called "similes," the second, "metaphors." Other figures of speech sometimes mentioned in textbooks seem to me either special kinds of metaphors ("personification," "metonymy," "synecdoche") or stylistic devices ("onomatopoea," "alliteration"). Possible exceptions are "antithesis" and "oxymoron," which in a way are the opposite of similes and metaphors, in that they bring together seemingly contradictory ideas.

really appropriate throughout? What kind of books, one wonders, are to be swallowed without chewing, and what happens to them if (as seems to be implied) they are not digested? Does even Bacon sometimes let his complacency at having invented a striking metaphor divert him from his main purpose? [8]

In Lyly, of course (to whom we should be grateful for his extreme examples), the imagery *is* the main purpose; to him, extravagance is a virtue. While Bacon's and Macaulay's figures of speech sometimes get out of hand, Lyly consciously delights in pushing them to excess. Most modern readers will feel that although comparing the effects of love and wine is natural and effective, Lyly's relentless pursuit of the comparison is not; that the metaphor is only a toy that the author for a moment wants to play with, not the expression of an insight that he wants to share.

And besides the danger that metaphor will become the end and not the instrument, the user runs another risk—that of abandoning one comparison before it is completed and instituting a different one. This is called a "mixed metaphor." Like a dangling modifier, a mixed metaphor involves an unconscious change in point of view, and the result can be equally incongruous. There is, for instance, Hamlet's famous debate with himself over whether "to take arms against a sea of troubles"—a picture a little hard to bring into focus, but saved from ridicule by reverence for the Bard. Such charity would hardly be extended to the college dean who in an inspirational address to an entering class exhorted them: "If you have the spark of genius burning in your souls, water it." Here a too exuberant fancy, seeking an apt comparison for genius, leaped from fire to flower, and the result was a mixing of metaphors whose initial impact is farcical—though a second and more sober response may see it as a somber forecast of what too often happens to college students.

The foregoing episode may be apocryphal, but my favorite example is authentic. The details are hazy after so many years, but in

---

[8] Originally I used a metaphor to comment on Bacon's metaphor: "let himself be seduced by the Sirens of rhetoric and forsake the austerity of truth." But then I asked myself how many readers would be familiar with Homer's story of Odysseus' encounter with the Sirens, and whether the "austerity of truth" would not sound too high-flown; whether the whole figure, in fact, might give the impression of being introduced for its own sake, even though it had occurred spontaneously. In the end I decided to retain it only in a footnote!

the congressional debate concerning membership in the United Nations, Senator John Bricker of Ohio proposed an amendment that would have drastically limited involvement by the United States; and the Chicago *Tribune,* its isolationist stance unaltered by World War II, declared in an editorial: "Now that the House has emasculated the Bricker Amendment, it is up to the Senate to restore its teeth."

But though metaphor may, like any other stylistic device, be sometimes abused, its forcefulness when aptly used is undeniable. It not only kindles the imagination; it satisfies, if only momentarily, the human mind's compulsive quest for unity amid the bewildering diversity of experience with which life confronts us.

8

BEAUTY

As imagery may play a major role in clarity and forcefulness, and still be natural, so it is often an intimate part of the fourth and final element to be considered in our analysis of style, namely, beauty. One hesitates, in this age of disillusionment, when many motion pictures and works of fiction are dominated by unredeemed human depravity—pictures that the actual behavior of men and women too often justifies—even to mention beauty. Yet no analysis of style, any more than of human experience as a whole, can afford to overlook it.

It is true that in much communication by means of words[1] it may appear irrelevant, and any effort to achieve it, misdirected. In day-to-day transactions of business, the only concern is that the record be clear; in friendly interchange of information and opinion, naturalness is the primary virtue; in more formal appearances at public meetings or in print, or even in private efforts at persuasion concerning some important current issue, it is forcefulness that is first sought.

Yet human life, after all, is more than business or social contacts, or political or intellectual conflict or accommodation. Those persons in history who have been most honored and revered were not military conquerors or rulers over vast areas or populations; or if they were, rarely, it is not their achievements in war and politics for which they have been accorded honor and reverence, but their

---

[1] I dare not say "verbal communication" for fear of being thought to refer only to *spoken* communication.

teaching, by example if not by discourse, that life's ultimate values are intangible.

One of these ultimate intangibles is beauty, in nature and in art. Emerson's simple tribute to the rhodora may or may not be regarded as poetically great or philosophically profound, but few poets or philosophers would deny that the affirmation in its most famous line is *true*—that "beauty is its own excuse for being." In writing, it is not, like clarity or naturalness or forcefulness, a means to an end but an end in itself.

It may, however, accompany and reinforce other intangible ends. These other ends would include the celebration—not, again, merely by praise, but by representation in true or imagined situations—of certain qualities or powers or achievements of the human spirit, in which is bound together, in Wordsworth's phrase, "the vast empire of human society, as it is spread over the whole earth, and over all time." And upon this unity of human experience rests the primary urge of the writer, in all but the most practical communication—informative or directive—to record and share the life of the mind: his perceptions, his convictions, his visions of what life is, or is about. The appeal of such a record, the success of such a sharing, lies partly in beauty of style.

It is true that not all authors of the past who are thought of as great, those possessed of powerful intellects or personalities or consummate skill as writers, have ever achieved, or perhaps cared to achieve, beauty of style. One thinks of Aristotle and Aquinas (as far as one can judge from translations) and Bacon, for all their depth and breadth of intellect; or Jonathan Swift, whose lucidity and passion place him beyond challenge in the highest rank of writers of English prose; or America's own folk-hero and world figure, master of many trades and arts, the possessor of immense personal charm and influence, an almost Olympian observer and actor in human affairs, Benjamin Franklin.

One may ask at this point what is meant by "beauty"? What is it that Plato's and Augustine's writings often have that Aristotle's and Aquinas's do not? What do we miss in the essays of Bacon that we find in the sermons of his contemporary, Donne? What is absent from Swift's work that is sometimes present in that of a lesser writer such as Richard Steele? Why do we not find in Franklin, the universal benefactor, the quality of style that is not denied to the passionate preacher of man's total depravity, Jonathan Edwards?

Perhaps these questions are in the end unanswerable because beauty is indefinable, though volumes have been written to bound and chart this country of the mind. Yet the urge to explore it still remains.

We can begin by saying that beauty of style is what gives pleasure by the way a thing is said, whether that thing is pleasant or unpleasant or neutral.[2] Next, seeking the source of this pleasure, we find it first perhaps in the sound of the separate words, and then by the way the words are linked by such aural devices as alliteration (the repetition of the same or similar consonants and the same or different vowels at the beginning of stressed syllables) and assonance (the repetition of the same vowel sound in conjunction with different consonants). These verbal harmonies may be enhanced by rhythm, a recurrent pattern (less regular than in traditional verse) of stressed and unstressed syllables, which in turn is often linked to such structural devices as parallelism and balance, or inversion of the natural English sentence order for the sake of emphasis.

This abstract analysis may gain clarity and substance from a passage of English prose that I first encountered in a college course in "advanced composition," and that remains in my memory after almost half a century. It is the closing paragraph of Bertrand Russell's essay "A Free Man's Worship."

> Brief and powerless is man's life. On him and all his race the slow sure doom falls pitiless and dark. Blind to good and evil, reckless of destruction, omnipotent matter rolls on its relentless way. For man, condemned today to lose his dearest, tomorrow himself to pass through the gate of darkness, it remains only to cherish, ere yet the night falls, the lofty thoughts that ennoble his little day. Disdaining the terrors of the coward slave of fate, to worship at the shrine that his own hands have built; undismayed by the empire of chance, to preserve a mind free from the tyranny that rules his outward life; proudly defiant of the irresistible forces that tolerate, for an instant, his knowledge and his condemnation, to sustain alone, a weary but un-

---

[2] If we try, however, to divorce words from meaning, to talk about words apart from what they say, we are no longer talking about language but about a form of music. A combination of words may be said to have beauty because it is agreeable in sound, but it cannot be said to constitute beauty of *style* unless it says something, unless it strikes the mind as well as the ear.

yielding Atlas, the world that his own ideals have fashioned despite the trampling march of unconscious power.

It is needless to dwell at length on Russell's brilliant use of the devices mentioned: alliteration ("slow sure doom . . . dark"); assonance ("lofty thoughts," "day; disdaining . . . slave . . . fate," "weary . . . unyielding . . . ideals"); parallelism ("blind . . . reckless . . . ," "disdaining . . . undismayed . . . defiant . . ."); inverted sentence order (suppose the first sentence were to read "Man's life is brief and powerless"). Less pervasive and obvious but not less effective is the imagery, limited here, as it happens, to metaphor ("the gate of darkness," "the . . . slave of fate," "the empire of chance," "a weary Atlas").

From this example one might conclude that intricacy of arrangement is essential to beauty of style. But this is not true. Beauty and simplicity need not be at odds. Even in poetry—and even in the work of an author so noted for the richness of his poetic art as Milton—some of the most moving passages are almost bare of ornament or artifice. One such passage is Manoa's valediction to his dead son in *Samson Agonistes*.

> Nothing is here for tears, nothing to wail
> Or knock the breast, no weakness, no contempt,
> Dispraise, or blame, nothing but well and fair,
> And what may quiet us in a death so noble.

It is true that despite the simplicity of the language the lines have a certain stateliness of movement, perhaps due to the presence of meter and the use of parallelism, which supplies the sole touch of studied art.

One can think of many other passages of verse where beauty goes hand in hand with simplicity; but, perhaps surprisingly, when we think of beauty in prose, it is usually of passages that are purple rather than plain. An exception (this one I encountered in graduate school) is a brief meditation by Sir William Temple, a minor statesman and author of the late seventeenth century, whose work embodies, like that of his near contemporaries Addison and Steele, the moderation and good sense of the age at its best.

> When all is done, human life is, at its greatest and best, but like a froward child, which must be humored and played with

a little to keep it quiet till it falls asleep, and then the care is over.

Here there seems to be no meticulous search for musical or emotion-laden words, no careful contrivance of elaborate rhythms, no reliance on unexpected or dramatic imagery. The single simile, though it takes up the whole sentence, is uncomplicated and unforced.

Moreover, the thought is not profound nor the feeling intense. There is neither the desperate idealism of "A Free Man's Worship" nor the sober certitude of "The Second Spring." Instead, there is an almost whimsical acceptance of a Lilliputian scale of human strivings and achievements, an almost light-hearted restatement of the somber conclusion of Ecclesiastes that "All is vanity."

One recalls, in contrast, Sir Walter Raleigh's famous apostrophe to death, which has a similar theme:

> O eloquent, just, and mighty Death! whom none could advise, thou hast persuaded; what none hath dared, thou hast done; and whom all the world hath flattered, thou only hast cast out of the world and despised; thou hast drawn together all the far-stretched greatness, all the pride, cruelty, and ambition of man, and covered it all over with these two narrow words: *Hic jacet!*

The beauty of this prose is apparent—the resounding words, the irresistible rhythm, the powerful emotion. But by the time of Temple, after a century of religious and civil strife, of fanaticism and disillusionment, these qualities of style had become suspect. Yet the later passage, also, has a claim to beauty that cannot be denied.

If beauty of style is unexpected in an age of rationalism and worldly wisdom, it is perhaps equally so in the work of an author who wrote almost two centuries later, in another country on another continent, about a kind of life as remote as can well be imagined from the ordered, polished, aristocratic society that we associate with the age to which Temple belonged. The author is Mark Twain, and the story is *Huckleberry Finn*. Moreover, since the story is told in the first person, and since Twain is an honest artist, the language is likewise worlds apart from that which is conventionally considered essential to beauty in writing. It is not only simple, it is almost totally innocent of the grammatical niceties that children of respectable parents were—and are—supposed to learn in school. But if some critic should suggest that the following passage is deprived of beauty by the "bad grammar," *I* would suggest that it is the critic and not Huck whose taste is corrupt.

> Well, when Tom and me got to the edge of the hilltop, we looked away down into the village and could see three or four lights twinkling, where there was sick folks, may be; and the stars over us was sparkling ever so fine; and down by the village was the river, a whole mile broad, and awful still and grand.

Twain, of course, is a genius, and even absolutists would perhaps excuse him for breaking the rules. But beauty of style is something to which grammar is irrelevant.

Nor is beauty the privilege of genius; it is sometimes within the reach of a college freshman, as in this description by one of my students of the writer's mother: "Her steps are slower now, but still she moves with grace; her shoulders now are stooped, but still she walks with pride."

Once more I resist the temptation to go on quoting. Instead, I heed the critic's conscience and ask again the inescapable question, "What is there in these passages that sets them apart from others that are also admirable, and gives them a valid claim to the special quality called beauty?

But, having asked the question, I have to answer that I do not know. Beauty is like the end of a rainbow; it is real but we can never grasp it. And while a physicist can tell us what a rainbow is and how it is created, there is no metaphysician who can do the same for beauty. To say that the quoted passages all produce a certain kind of pleasurable feeling (some of my young friends might say, "Good vibes!") is to beg the question.

If, however, it is permissible to let fancy play with possibilities, without committing oneself to defense or argument, I suggest that what is common to the passages, infinitely various in style and substance, that we call beautiful, is a certain tone (I can find no fitter word) that arises from the union, on the one hand, of an arrangement of words that for most readers will have the charm of music, and, on the other hand, a specific thought or feeling or vision that stirs an echo of acknowledgement in other hearts and minds. It may be the need of trust in the self, as in Russell; or in something beyond the self, as in Newman; or the tragic recognition, in Raleigh, of the sovereign power of death; or the escape from tragedy, as in

Temple, through a compassionate and only half sad acceptance of the frailty of human life; or, as in Twain, the unsophisticated awe of an opening mind in the presence of natural beauty, tempered by a sense of kinship with humble human life (the sparkling stars above are balanced by the twinkling lights below "where there was sick folks, may be"); or my student's thoughtful and profound reverence for a mother worthy of such filial regard.

On this note, these reflections on the nature of beauty of style might end. But something still asks for expression concerning both the music and the meaning whose union gives birth to beauty. Though the question of why this quality is missing from the work of some of the greatest writers of English prose was earlier put aside as impossible to answer, perhaps a little more reflection will light us a little farther on the pathway to the unattainable.

A first tentative suggestion is that beauty in writing demands a love of language for its own sake; not, to be sure, to the point of ignoring thought and feeling, for then we get Euphuism or some other empty form, but as a legitimate companion of the idea or emotion that the author wishes to share. Perhaps one trouble with such authors as Bacon, Swift, and Franklin is that their concern with content leads them for the most part to regard language only as an instrument. The result is that the primary virtues of their writing are clarity and force; from their point of view, beauty is at best a luxury, at worst an impediment.

But, as a second suggestion, in the work of these authors something is missing from the content, all-important as it is assumed to be. What keeps Bacon's work from being fully satisfying to some readers may be the lack of feeling—the banishment of emotion by intellect. He does indeed, in his dissection of human nature, acknowledge the power of irrational urges, but he views them always from the outside, without a hint that he himself has ever been thus stirred. That anyone should have found it possible to credit him with having written Shakespeare's plays, whose author is able to empathize with an infinite variety of human passions, is surely one of the minor mysteries of the universe. As it is obvious that Shakespeare surpasses Bacon in his love for language, it is still more obvious that his work is animated by far deeper feeling.

No one can accuse Jonathan Swift, however, of lacking feeling. Beneath the easy flow of seeming fact and common sense—the "modest proposal," for instance, to cure Ireland's economic and social ills by selling babies for food—there seethes a fury that many critics have viewed as pathological. This fury is aroused by the folly, vanity, treachery, and cruelty which in Swift's vision dominate the behavior of the human race. Yet it does not seem to be inspired, as in most sensitive persons it would be, by pity for the victims; it is a kind of abstract hatred of a race of creatures who are capable of reason but refuse to act reasonably. No allowance is made for human weakness, no account is taken of the complexity of human motives, no recognition is accorded, as in Christianity (though Swift was an Anglican clergyman) to the possibility of repentance and forgiveness. May one entertain the hypothesis that the absence of beauty in Swift's writing—which in clarity, naturalness, and forcefulness is beyond all praise—is at least partly the result of his profound alienation from all but a handful of his fellow human beings?

The case of Franklin is perhaps the most curious. We know that he, too, was capable of passion; that the sweet—or at least amiable—reasonableness that pervades the *Autobiography* did not invariably rule his actual life. Even in the studied detachment of that narrative, one can read between the seemingly ingenuous lines the story of personal relationships that were sometimes stormy and bitter, along with those that were smooth and pleasant. Moreover, in regard to impersonal issues, his generally complacent worldliness is not incompatible with unstinted devotion to an ideal, to a cause in which mere prudence would have told him "not to get involved." In supporting the Revolution he recognized that if the leaders did not hang together (few revolutionists have done so), they all, including himself, might be hanged separately for treason. It is relevant to add (lest we forget the musical partner in the marriage) that besides the richness of his life and character in relations with his fellow human beings, Franklin was not without a sense of beauty. He invented, in fact, a musical instrument, the glass harmonica, for which Mozart did not disdain to write a composition. So one may wonder why there is so little music in the style, as there is so little passion in the substance, of his work.

One answer that occurs is that in his writings he was unable, or unwilling, to let himself go. If he ever felt inspired by some power outside himself, he evidently refused to surrender to it. If his sympathy for his fellows threatened to get out of hand, it would seem that he resolutely restrained it. The ideal of moral perfection that he outlines in his *Autobiography* allows for no irrational conduct; indeed, his matter-of-fact pursuit of such a goal, the very notion that such an achievement is possible, involves the renunciation of any kind of unconditional commitment. In set of mind, it is almost antithetical to that involved in the pursuit of beauty in writing, namely, an absolute trust in one's feelings—toward language and toward life— and an unquestioning faith in the responsiveness of at least some of the persons for whom one writes.[3]

This faith, one may suggest, is part of that great intangible that Joseph Conrad spoke of as "human solidarity"; or (to exercise the "unchartered freedom" that I spoke for at the beginning of this analysis) of what the King James Version of the New Testament calls "charity," and the Revised Version "love"—the outrageously irrational assumption of the spiritual unity of humanity. If this assumption is accepted, then what goes into beauty of style is not only a love of words but (in some sense) a love of persons.

Having mentioned Conrad, I will end this chapter with a quotation that I still cherish more, after half a century devoted to the study and teaching of literary masterpieces, than any other passage in English prose. It comes at the point in *Lord Jim* where the unnamed narrator, retired from his roaming of Eastern seas, receives from Marlow a manuscript containing the final chapters of Jim's story. I offer it unburdened by analysis.

> The light of his shaded reading lamp slept like a sheltered pool, his footfalls made no sound on the carpet, his wandering days were over. No more horizons as boundless as hope, no more twilights within the forests as solemn as temples, in the hot quest for the ever undiscovered country over the hill, across the stream, beyond the wave. The hour was striking! no more, no more! but the opened packet under the lamp brought back the sounds, the visions, the very savor of the past. A multitude of fading faces, a tumult of low voices dying away upon the shores of distant seas, under a passionate and unconsoling sunshine. He sighed and sat down to read.

---

[3] As a sometime scholar in certain areas (though not, generally speaking, in those involved in the present work!), I am impelled by a scholar's conscience, as well as by common prudence, to confess that I am not an "expert" on Bacon, Swift, and Franklin, and that my interpretations of their work may be challenged by persons with a more intimate knowledge of their lives and writings. But even if the illustrations are rejected, the general principles may still be valid.

EPILOGUE

On Teaching and Learning the Use of English Prose

As one who thinks of himself as being, or having been, before all else a teacher of composition, I cannot comfortably end this essay without some reflections about how one learns to write. Throughout the preceding pages, in fact, there has been implicit the hope that they would help some readers not only to a better understanding than they had before of how their language works and of what a good prose style involves, but to an examination of their own use of language, especially in writing.

At the same time, I concur with the authors of *Research in Written Composition*[1] that nobody knows exactly how students, and other persons, improve their writing. And I certainly do not intend in the following comments to adopt an absolutist stance. Although they reflect the experience of many years of trying to help students to write well (and to learn the art myself), I know no way to prove them valid.

Still, for one thing, common sense suggests that, as in acquiring any other skill, like playing a musical instrument, practice is the first essential; one learns to write by *writing*. It is true that some persons have a natural facility in the use of words, as others have in music or mathematics, but these talents, like those in the Gospel, are worthless unless increased by use, by honest and arduous effort. Reading about how to write, or talking about it, does not bring

---

[1] See p. 56 above.

automatic improvement. School or college courses in which students are supposed to gain a measure of writing skill, but in which little or no writing is done, are a fraud. Conclusions that are presented in texts or lectures, or that evolve from class discussion, must be applied, consciously and regularly, in the student's own work.

Likewise, "work-book" exercises, involving revision of out-of-context sentences, are more likely to profit the author and the publisher than the student. Even classroom correction of faulty passages from students' own papers, though it can be fun, is of value only if the writers get a chance, while the experience is still fresh, to apply in practice what they may have learned.

This practice, it should be added, differs from that which is essential in some other types of activity in that technique cannot be separated from substance. Mechanical exercises, which are helpful to beginning typists or musicians, are irrelevant to the process of learning to write. That is, good writing is always writing *about something*, and practice is of value only when the writer feels that what he is trying to say is worth the effort.

In this fact lies the great problem of "Freshman Composition" in college, and presumably in high school courses in composition as well. Most students have—or think they have—nothing that they want to say, and they are right in feeling that being forced to write on topics concerning which they have little knowledge and less interest is a waste of time.

The key to better writing, then, is "motivation," and the primary task of the teacher of composition is to make students feel that they have something to say, some experience that they wish to share. But the power thus to inspire them is not a mechanical procedure, and there are no rules that guarantee success. The truth is, unwelcome as the implications are for those who naturally would like to think that skill in teaching can be taught, that the ability to make students want to write is an individual gift, possessed by different persons in varying degree.

Another difficulty is raised by cynics who assert—on the whole, truly—that even if students can be brought to the point of wanting to say something, what they will want to say is likely to be trite and superficial. But a more realistic as well as more generous view is that this situation is both inevitable and—hopefully—temporary. It is obviously unfair to expect high school students or college freshmen to arrive at opinions that are original or profound. What

EPILOGUE

is important is that *they* have a sense of intellectual advance, and that it is justified. We who find their views naive forget that everybody must start somewhere, and that at one time our opinions were equally superficial and simplistic.

This does not mean that the teacher must be uncritical. The student who has honestly tried, first, to get his thoughts clear in his own mind, and then to communicate them to his reader, deserves to have them taken seriously; and this means that the teacher, while giving credit for an honest effort, must point out flaws in content as well as form; perhaps unsupported generalizations or too great reliance upon a single instance or a single source. And beyond this, he must challenge beliefs or attitudes—such as racism or ultranationalism or docile acceptance of some set of economic dogmas—that lead to social strife rather than to social harmony. (Though I put the argument here on a pragmatic basis, I confess to being, on a few moral issues—though only a few—an absolutist.) It is wrong, of course, and often "counterproductive" (I like this newly coined term) to try to force one's own opinions on one's students. But it is right to try to make them self-critical, to help them develop the habit of scrutinizing their own work, searching out and removing faults and weaknesses in the content of their compositions.

Self-criticism is also the key to excellence of style. It is true that clarity, naturalness, forcefulness, and beauty are unquestionable virtues of style (though one of them must sometimes be balanced against another); but the writer himself must be the judge as to when these virtues have been realized. I have always (at least in later years, and I hope even when I was young and self-assured) told a student who defended his way of saying something, against my adverse criticism: "Well, you have to say it the way *you* think is best; there's no point in trying to say it the way *I* think is best. The important thing is that you ask yourself what the best way is."

Until this habit of self-criticism has been acquired, however, the student learns little from writing compositions that are not read and criticized by a competent and conscientious instructor. He may, in fact, even strengthen some bad habits. Writing (once more) is not a mechanical skill, and I have never asked a student to write a paper that I did not intend to read.

I naturally think in terms of teacher and student, but of course one need not go to college to learn to write well. Every school child of my generation, at least in Massachusetts, learned that Abraham

EPILOGUE

Lincoln had only a few months of formal schooling. In high school we learned from Franklin's *Autobiography* that he was self-educated after the age of eight. And when we read *Moby Dick,* we found Melville asserting that "a whale-ship was my Harvard College and my Yale."

These and a host of lesser writers had, however, the motivation that contemporary college students often lack. They understood that mastery of the English language was a means to the achievement of their various goals, and no one had to require them to practice writing or to urge them to be self-critical.

They were also, as a matter of course, well read. And here is another problem for the contemporary teacher of composition. An instructor can inculcate, in some students, at least, the *habit* of self-criticism, but he cannot, except to a limited degree, supply the *basis* for it. This must come mainly from what a person reads, and to a lesser degree from what he hears. And many young people today, even those who aspire to a college degree, have neither read nor heard much English of a kind to give them a feeling for the language and for its possibilities as an instrument of communication. I once had a student who, in writing about the topic "The Kind of Reading I Like Best," chose with commendable honesty or perhaps naiveté to write about comic books, and the fact must be regretfully recorded that his favorite reading was reflected in his style. Similarly, one would not expect a boy (or girl, I must remember to add) whose reading was mainly about sports to possess a vocabulary adequate for the discussion of philosophy or politics, nor perhaps much sensitivity to shadings of meaning or subtleties of sentence movement. Still less is probably to be expected of one who spends his leisure in front of a TV set;[1] though network newscasts are usually literate, and possess in particular the virtues of clarity and economy, and a number of special programs expose the viewer and listener to decent, and occasionally distinguished, prose.

Good writing, then, it seems obvious, depends upon good reading. It is from reading that we acquire a vocabulary expressive of the fine distinctions of thought and feeling that are essential to the

[1] I have noted that more and more frequently a television set is referred to simply as "a television." Though I have still not got fully accustomed to it, I have to agree that it is convenient, and I do not see that any confusion results from treating "television," like "radio," as a term both for a medium of communication and for the instrument that is used.

EPILOGUE

sharing of any but the most simple experience. It is from reading that we get a feeling for rhythm and stress, and a resultant skill in fashioning sentences whose form intensifies the impact of their content. To take the obvious example, it is hard to name a famous writer in the English language whose style has not been influenced by his reading of the English Bible—which is literally a closed book to recent generations, except for selections that may be included in courses in "World Literature" and in which students are likely to have no more than a casual interest at best.

Some authors have recorded their efforts to improve their style by the deliberate imitation of selected models: Franklin, for instance, with *The Spectator*, and Stevenson with the early seventeenth-century masters of English prose. In these instances, certainly, the method was successful. But perhaps most persons would find such discipline more tedious than profitable; and their feeling for language, their taste in using it, is an unconscious by-product of reading done for other ends—for information, perhaps, or simply pleasure. The type of reading does not really matter; it may be fiction, history, biography, philosophy, informal essays, the writings of critics and columnists; it may include the august voices of the past, like those chosen for quotation in the present work, or those whose accent and idiom are of our own time.

One may suggest, in fact, that what is read is less important than how the reading is done. In the end, indeed, the latter may determine the former. For just as one who seeks excellence in his own writing must learn to be self-critical, so in his reading he must be clear-eyed and clear-minded, scrutinizing and judging the style as well as the substance, rightly resentful of language that is dull or obscure or prolix or pompous, even though the value of the content demands that he go on reading; grateful for a vocabulary that is vivid and precise, for sentences that focus his attention on the crucial points in the action or the argument.

This way of reading obviously demands a measure of deliberation. "Speed reading," in contrast, though useful in acquiring facts, has limitations that its advocates naturally do not dwell upon. It permits no awareness of style (and, what is irrelevant here but even more serious, no critical analysis of argument or opinion). One gets no sense of what the words would sound like, no associations, no awareness of the stresses and rhythms that add to the literal meaning and enhance the author's intent. It may be said, in fact, that except for matter that is purely informational or fiction whose only function is to rest the mind, anything that is worth reading, is worth reading slowly.

I would even suggest, as an aid in learning how to muster for one's own purposes the full resources of the English language, the memorizing of passages of prose and poetry that strike one as having particular appeal, and the repetition of these, silently or vocally, in otherwise mentally idle moments. One thus acquires a feeling for the language that the most painstaking analysis can never confer. (It is also a never-failing source of pleasure in an existence where such sources are always welcome.) It has sometimes occurred to me, indeed, that classes in "Remedial English" would be more profitable to the reluctant enrollees if, instead of the customary "drill in fundamentals," the time was devoted to reading aloud or hearing on records notable passages of English prose, or even verse. Only, one is paralyzed by a sense of futility at having only three hours a week for one semester in which to compensate for years of indifference or misdirected effort.

Finally, what goes into good writing—besides a natural gift, besides having something to say, besides long and thoughtful practice, besides a feeling for words and sentences that has come from wide and reflective reading—is simply *work*. It is true that sometimes, if we are lucky, the right word, the ringing phrase, will come uncalled for; there are times, even, when words and thoughts seem to combine of themselves, and the writer need only hasten to record the result, though perhaps in the cold light of a later reading the combinations may seem less inevitable.

But mostly, success in writing results from the patient—or impatient but nevertheless persistent—groping for the exact word, the telling phrase, the sentence shape that will be clear and forceful, the image that will be both striking and natural, the order of presentation that will be most logical and emphatic. The resources of the English language are equal to the task of expressing whatever is permitted by the nature of language itself. But the mastery of these resources can come only from unremitting effort.

Whether such effort is worth while is properly a matter of personal choice. But it is proper, in making the choice, to be clear concerning the benefits as well as the cost. The benefit commonly alleged in our society, as being that which is most widely desired, is greater financial wealth, or power, or prestige. It is not apparent,

EPILOGUE

however, that those persons who arrive at the top in politics or business are in general notably superior in their use of language to many who occupy less eminent positions—or that they need to be. Conventional correctness is no doubt important; but precision, force, and felicity are the rare and seemingly ineffectual possession of an Adlai Stevenson. I would hesitate to promise a student that skill in writing would confer what is commonly thought of as "success."

One can, however, give some assurance of less tangible rewards. One of these is the satisfaction of knowing what one thinks—which is not as common or easy as is sometimes assumed. No other discipline is so effective in clarifying a person's opinions, and his reasons for holding them, as the process of putting them into words. (Having some one else write one's speeches or other statements, if these contain more than platitudes or slogans or ceremonial vacuities, is to have some one else do one's thinking.) The common plea of students, "I know it but I can't say it," though not as a rule intentionally evasive, is less than wholly true; they have, one often feels, not *tried* to say it. And those who are not satisfied with mere dogma or supposition, who wish to know what assumptions and what evidence have led to their conclusions—the conclusion, for instance, that abortion is or is not a crime, or that bigness in business is or is not an evil—can resolve their doubts and confirm their faith in no other way than by putting into words, completely and exactly, their feelings and thoughts.

And in the process one becomes a more complete human being. It was the judgment of the French philosopher and naturalist Buffon that "style is the man himself." [2] And Milton averred that "he who would not be frustrate of his hope to write well hereafter in laudable things, ought himself to be a true poem." It is certainly true that what a person *is* determines how he writes or speaks. But the converse is also true, at least in part. In the struggle to give clear and natural and forceful and sometimes beautiful expression to one's experience, one becomes a more honest and genuine and decisive and imaginative person. To increase one's sensitivity to

[2] I do not know whether Women's Liberation has caused the same pointless problems in the use of the French "l'homme" as in the use of the English "man." Once more I affirm my unqualified belief in equal rights for women, but I resent as irrelevant and disruptive the effort to force the English language into unfamiliar molds.

language as a medium of expression of human experience is to increase one's sensitivity to the experience itself. Anyone who tries (to take one of many examples that crowd forward) to the utmost of his ability to express in words his love of nature, of a person, of an institution, or of an ideal will find his love inevitably strengthened.

And finally, there is implicit in the act of communication—which is what the use of language *is*—the recognition of a bond with other persons, of some kind of community of which one is a member, with whose other members one wishes to share his experience. This is the central fact of human existence—that any existence properly called "human" can be achieved only within a community. A being in physical human form who could somehow survive without contact with human society would possess not even the power of speech. We do not learn by ourselves but always from others—by imitating, by listening, by reading, or by observing and drawing conclusions as we have been taught to do. All our goals and all our values, our very identities, are derived, directly or indirectly, from the community—or communities, since each is part of a series in which the units are progressively more inclusive—to which we belong.

At the same time, however, we have arrived by some unknown way at the notion of the infinite value of the individual, unique and self-directed. The community that we think of as "human" does not exist by compulsion or by the apparently mindless drives that govern the behavior of ants and bees, but by the conscious recognition and acceptance of mutual benefits and obligations, tangible and intangible, between individuals and between the individual and the community.

The quality of these relationships, the strength of these bonds, and the widening of both that is imperative if our race is to be saved from self-destruction, depends at least in part on success in communication, in the sharing of experience by means of words. In the mastery of this art, therefore, is to be found not only a greater measure of self-realization, of knowledge and freedom, than is possible to the person who is unlettered, but closer and warmer and more sustaining ties with our fellow pilgrims on the particular road that it has been our destiny or choice to follow; and ultimately, though perhaps in ways not yet visible or demonstrable, with other passengers on this spaceship Earth.

INDEX

"Absolutist," defined, 17
Addison, Joseph, 69n., 123
"Afflict-inflict, 72
Agnew, Spiro, 101
"Ain't," 7, 8, 10, 18, 32
Alliteration, 122, 123
American Heritage Dictionary Usage Panel, i, 22n., 23–24, 26, 29, 71n., 73n., 74n., 86, 100
Amherst *Record*, 72
Aquinas, Saint Thomas, 121
Areopagitica, see Milton, John
Aristotle, 121
Arnold, Matthew, 112n.
Assonance, 122, 123
Audubon magazine, 72, 100
Augustine, Saint, 121

Bacon, Francis, 114–115, 117–118, 121, 126, 128n.
Baker, Russell, 52n.
Baker, Sheridan, 17n., 52n., 101, 112n.
Bartley, David, 65n.
Barzun, Jacques, 52n.
Beauclerk, Topham, 31
Bentham, Jeremy, 26
Bernstein, Theodore, 52n.
Bible, the, 39–40, 133; King James Version, 43, 47–48, 51, 61, 62, 80, 128
Bishop, Morris, 24, 29
"Black English," 32–35

Blackmur, R. P., 103–104
Boston *Globe*, ii, 21, 60, 65n., 66, 71, 72, 74, 100
Boswell, James, 30
Bradlee, Benjamin, 65n.
Bricker, John, 119
Browne, Sir Thomas, 72n.
Browning, Robert, 112n.
Buckley, William F., Jr., 52n.
Buffon, de, Comte Georges Louis Leclerc, 135
Burpee Seed Company, 74

"Cannot help but," 100–101
"Center around," 26–27
Charles I, 108
Chesterfield, Philip Dormer Stanhope, Earl of, 31
Chicago *Tribune*, 90, 119
Churchill, Winston, 5, 101
Clemens, Samuel, see Mark Twain
Cleveland *Plain Dealer*, 10
Cleveland *Press*, 11
Coherence, 92–96
College English, 34n.
Communication, the function of language, 16, 18–19
Comparative degree of adjectives, see Superlative degree
Concreteness, 84, 87–88, 108–109
Conrad, Joseph, 87, 89, 128
"Contact," 26

INDEX

Content words, 42
"Convince-persuade," 70
Coping, see Moynihan, Daniel P.
Crisis, The, see Paine, Thomas
"Criteria," 73–74
Curme, George O., 112n.

Dangling modifiers, 89–91
"Data," 74
"Decimate," 72
Dickinson, Emily, 98
"Different than," 17, 20n., 98–99
"Distinterested-uninterested," 21–22, 60, 70
Donne, John, 49, 121
"Down," superfluous use of, 27–28
Dukakis, Michael, 65n.

Ecclesiastes, 124
Edwards Johnathan, 121
Elizabeth, Queen Mother, 5
Emerson, Ralph Waldo, 55, 121
Emphasis, 92, 106, 109–112
"Enormity," 72–73
Euphues, see Lyly, John
"Everybody" as plural, 54–55

Fadiman, Clifton, 12
Faulkner, William, 18, 82–83
Figures of Speech, see Imagery
"Finalize," 26
"Flaunt-flout," 21, 70
Follett, Wilson, 24–25, 47, 71n., 101
Formal English, 29–32
For Whom the Bell Tolls, see Hemingway, Ernest
Foster Parents Plan, 49
Fowler, H. W., 24
Franklin, Benjamin, 121, 126, 127–128 and n., 132, 133
"Free Man's Worship, A." see Russell, Bertrand
Freud, Sigmund, 58
Function words, 42
"Fundamentals," 14

"Gay," 73
"Gladiolus," variant forms of, 74–75

Goldsmith, Oliver, 30
Gove, Philip, 23
Grammar, definition of, 40; _____and anatomy, a false analogy, 56
Grammatical forms, 40ff.; nouns, 40, 42–43; pronouns, 43–45; verbs, 41, 45–46
Growth and Structure of the English Language, The, see Jesperson, Otto
Guide to American English, see Myers, L. M.
Gulliver's Travels, see Swift, Jonathan

Hamlet, 48, 49, 62–63, 101, 118
Heath, Edward, 107
Hemingway, Ernest, 9, 82, 83, 113–114
Holiday magazine, 12
Holmes, Oliver Wendell, 112n.
"Hopefully," 102
Huckleberry Finn, see Mark Twain

"I" as object, 26, 29
"I-me," 52–54
Imagery, 116–119, 123; classified, 117n.
"Imply-infer," 22, 70
"Increbile-incredulous," 71
Index to English, see Perrin, Porter G.
Inflections, see Grammatical forms
"Inflict," see "Afflict-inflict"
Informal English, see Formal English
In Our Time, see Hemingway, Ernest
International Wildlife, 75
"Interpersonal," 34n.

James, William, 26
Jesperson, Otto, 47n.
Johnson, Samuel, 5, 7, 23, 30–31, 75–76, 108, 109
Julius Caesar, 62

Kennedy, Edward 65 and n., 71
Kennedy, John F., 65n.
Kissinger, Henry, 69n.

Langton, Bennett, 31
Lawrence, D. H., 100
Levels of usage, 28ff.

INDEX

Life of Johnson, see Boswell, James
Light in August, see Faulkner, William
"Like-as," 99–100
Lincoln, Abraham, 131–132
Lindsay, John, 21
Loose sentences, 111
Lord Jim, see Conrad, Joseph
Lyly, John, 112–113, 114, 115, 117

MacArthur, Douglas, 48
Macaulay, Thomas B., 115–116, 118
Macbeth, 62
MacPherson, James, 109
Mark Twain, 124–125, 126
Marx, Karl, 34n.
"Maximize," 25–26
"May-might," 64–65
McLuhan, Marshall, 13
Mearns, Hughes, 53
"Media," 74
Melman, Seymour, 107, 108 and n.
Melville, Herman, 132
Merchant of Venice, The, 54
Metaphor, see Imagery
Milton, John, 108–109, 123, 135
Mixed metaphors, 118–119
Modern American Usage, see Follett, Wilson
Modern English Usage, see Fowler, H. W.
Morality and language, 8–10
Morse, J. Mitchell, 34n., 57, 92
Moyers, Bill, 65
Moynihan, Daniel P., 86, 87n.
Myers, L. M., 24n.

National Council of Teachers of English, 56
National Lawyers Guild, 21
Newman, Edwin, 11n., 104, 107
Newman, John Henry, 16, 116, 124, 125
New Yorker, The, 12, 53, 56, 57
New York Times, ii. 3, 22, 72, 74
New York Times Book Review, 70, 72–73, 100, 108
New York Times Magazine, 4, 10, 52

Nigger of the Narcissus, The, see Conrad, Joseph
Nixon, Richard, 21, 87, 97, 111
"Nobody" and "none" as plural, 55–56

Oedipus the King, 58
"Oral-verbal," 70–71
Othello, 50
Oxford English Dictionary, 22n, 71n.

Paine, Thomas, 5
Parallelism, 112–116, 122, 123
Past tense, replacing pluperfect and present perfect, 66–67
Pater, Walter, 112n.
Paul VI, Pope, 58, 71
Periodic sentences, 111
Permanent War Economy, The, see Melman, Seymour
Perrin, Porter G., 24n.
"Persuade," see "Convince-persuade"
Planned Parenthood League of Massachusetts, 21
Plato, 121
Poems of Ossian, 30
Pope, Alexander, 90, 91
Practical Stylist, The, see Baker, Sheridan
"Pragmatic," defined, 17
Preposition ending a sentence, 101–102
Pronouns, vague reference of, 91

Raleigh, Walter, 124
Ready and Easy Way to Establish a Free Commonwealth, A, see Milton, John
Reagan, Ronald, 21
"Reason is because," 98
"Repel-repulse," 71
Research in Written Composition, 56, 129
Roberts, Paul, 39
Roosevelt, Eleanor, 5
Ruskin, John, 112n.
Russell, Bertrand, 122-123, 124, 125

INDEX

Samson Agonistes, see Milton John
"Second Spring, The," see Newman, John Henry
Shakespeare, 54, 61, 62, 63, 71n., 101, 126; see also *Hamlet, Macbeth, Merchant of Venice, Othello*
"Shall-will," 47–49
Simile, see Imagery
Simplicity, in choice of words, 85–87; excessive, in sentence structure, 113–114
Slaughterhouse Five, see Vonnegut, Kurt
Smith, Lillian, 8
Sons and Lovers, see Lawrence, D. H.
Speed reading, 133
"Standard" English, 34–35, 37
Steele, Richard, 121, 123
Stevenson, Robert Louis, 133
Strange Fruit, see Smith, Lillian
"Strata," 74
Stravinsky, Igor, 69n.
Strictly Speaking, see Newman, Edwin
Strong verbs, 45–46
Subjunctive mood, 68–69, 98
Sun Also Rises, The, see Hemingway, Ernest
Superlative degree of adjective, replacing comparative degree, 67–68
Supreme Court of the United States, 7, 18, 61

Swift, Jonathan, 88, 121, 126–127, 128n.

"Take for granite," 27
Temple, William, 123–124, 126

"Uninterested," see "Disinterested-uninterested"
United Press, 3, 4
Unity, 92
"Up," superfluous use of, 27–28 and n.
Upward mobility, 37

Vietnam war, 89, 91
Virgil, 58
"Verbal," see "Oral-verbal"
Vonnegut, Kurt, 9

Warton, Thomas, 31
Watergate, 65, 97, 111
Webster, Noah, 22n., 69n., 70n., 100
Webster's Collegiate Dictornary, 86
Webster's Third New International Dictionary, i, 5, 23, 61, 71n.
White, E. B., 12
"Who-whom," 49–52, 98
"Will," see "Shall-will"
Women's Liberation, 7, 20n., 135n.
Wordiness, 106–108
Wordsworth, William, 20, 121
"Would of," 27
Writer's Guide, see Perrin, Porter G.

Library of Congress Cataloging in Publication Data
Barnard, Ellsworth, 1907–
English for everybody.
Includes index.
 1. English language—Usage. 2. English language—Style. I. Title.
PE1460.B375   420   79-18238